"I don't know what I love most about Courtney Zoffness's *Spilt Milk*. The taut originality of the prose? The acuity of its insights? The daring vulnerability? There are so many things I want to say about *Spilt Milk*, but, honestly, they're all variations of *This is fucking brilliant*. Whatever you think this book is, it's more. A debut writer this talented and skilled is an event in itself."

—Mat Johnson, author of *Pym*

"Gentle, playful, and laced with subtle wit, these essays are a welcome balm in an insane and un-gentle time."

—Mary Gaitskill, author of *Bad Behavior* and *This Is Pleasure*

"Courtney Zoffness is a gorgeous writer with that rarest of qualities: heart. *Spilt Milk* contains the wisdom of a mother, the maturity of an older sister, and the wide-eyed wonder of a small child. It's a magical gift of a collection."

—Lisa Taddeo, author of *Three Women*

"These bright, knowing essays spill over with intelligence and wit. Courtney Zoffness traces the dizzying conflict faced by parents—the daily ricochet between burden and joy—and, with a sharply lyric voice, discovers hidden connections between this domestic struggle and the larger cultural and political winds shifting around us."

—Ben Marcus, author of *Notes from the Fog*

"On one level, *Spilt Milk* is an extraordinary exploration of the connections—small and large, real and imagined—between childhood and parenthood. On another level, it's irrefutable proof that Courtney Zoffness is a wondrous calculus of a prose writer: keen, inventive, candid, charitable, not to mention one helluva stylist."

—Mitchell S. Jackson, author of *Survival Math*

"Wry and masterful, *Spilt Milk* examines the multiplicities of self and culture, asking the tough questions with remarkable concision. Courtney Zoffness is a writer of supernatural acuity and wit."
—T Kira Madden, author of *Long Live the Tribe of Fatherless Girls*

"*Spilt Milk* is current, self-examining, self-aware, honest, insightful, biting, and funny. Essentially, it's a perfect book."
—Jesse Eisenberg, actor and author of
Bream Gives Me Hiccups and Other Stories

"Courtney Zoffness's collection is written with a fierce and often funny honesty. Zoffness explores motherhood and daughterhood and how these early attachments make us and unmake us, how they connect us to others—until they are us."
—Tiphanie Yanique, author of *Land of Love and Drowning*

"In these ten musical, open-hearted essays, Courtney Zoffness establishes herself as one of our most soulful, clear-eyed narrators. A lucid dream of a book I wished would never end."
—Elisa Albert, author of *After Birth*

SPILT MILK

McSWEENEY'S
SAN FRANCISCO

Copyright © 2021 by Courtney Zoffness

Versions of some essays in this book first appeared in the following: "Hot for Teacher" in *Indelible in the Hippocampus: Writings from the Me Too Movement*; "Holy Body" in the *Southern Review*; "It May All End in Aleppo" in *Arts & Letters*; "Black Forest," as "Up in the Trees," in *Indiana Review*; "Trespass," as "Spilt Milk," in the *Paris Review Daily*.

All rights reserved, including right of reproduction in whole or in part, in any form.

McSweeney's and colophon are registered trademarks of McSweeney's, an independent publisher based in San Francisco.

ISBN: 978-1-952119-14-9

10 9 8 7 6 5 4 3 2 1

www.mcsweeneys.net

Printed in Canada

SPILT MILK

MEMOIRS

COURTNEY ZOFFNESS

McSWEENEY'S
SAN FRANCISCO

CONTENTS

A *mame hot oygen fun gloz.*
(A mother has eyes of glass.)
　　　　　　　—Yiddish proverb

"If we are lucky, the end of the sentence
is where we might begin. If we are
lucky, something is passed on, another
alphabet written in the blood, sinew,
and neuron; ancestors charging their
kin with the silent propulsion to fly
south, to turn toward the place in the
narrative no one was meant to outlast."
　　　　　　　　　—Ocean Vuong

For Jeremy

THE ONLY THING
WE HAVE TO FEAR

HERE IS MY OLDEST son, age five, at not quite 6 a.m.:

I can't go to school! His eyes are wild, lidless.

I wrench out the worry like a splinter: His schoolmates have learned new things and he won't be able to follow. We've been out of town. He has missed Monday's class.

I rub his back, offer reassurances. Maybe you'll feel better after breakfast, I say.

When I head to the kitchen, he slams his bedroom door, bars himself inside. Don't make me go!

Mommy and Daddy would never suggest you do something that's a bad idea, I say—and wonder if it's true.

He barely removes the thumb from his mouth as I pull a shirt over his head. I lure him out of the house with a lollipop. Midway into the six-minute walk, his panic mounts.

What time is it? he says. Am I late? He takes off down the sidewalk.

Honey, you're not late, I call. I catch up with him at the intersection, a network of strollers and scooters and clasped hands. He is doubled over.

I have to poop, he says.

School's across the street. We'll go to the second-floor bathroom, I say.

No, he screams, and stamps his feet. He is wearing light-up shoes.

We drift upstairs with the crowd, and I report him present to his teacher while he twists beside me in visceral discomfort. He agrees to use the toilet only if I wait outside the bathroom, but any relief I feel over this deal dissipates when he reemerges seconds later, pants at his ankles.

I don't have to go anymore, he says, zipping up his fly.

Are you sure? Want to just sit for a minute and see?

I can't, he says, and hurries to class.

Later he will tell my husband that he was secretly sobbing in bed before he called out to us that morning, that he knew it was silly but couldn't stop.

A memory. My brother and I sourcing scrap wood from the yard of a home that has recently burned down. We want to build a tree house. I spot a square just the right size for a floor, but it turns out that in the blaze, the lawn has transmuted into thick, sticky mud, and it suctions my shoes, envelops my calves. A few yards away, my brother is swallowed up to his knees. He screams. I'm older, the designated protector. Panic saturates my chest. And then, as if only to test my tolerance, a blue van pulls up.

Kidnappers drive blue vans. We have been warned to steer clear.

A pale man with a splotchy beard pokes his head out the window. Can I help?

We are perfect prey, stuck in a muddy trap on a quiet cul-de-sac around the corner from home, out of our parents' view.

I holler and squirm and somehow tug off my shoes and force my way to the dry edge of the property. I am crying. My brother is bawling.

Young lady, the man repeats. Need help?

I need my father, but retrieving him will mean leaving my brother alone with a strange man. My brother is heaving so hard that I can't understand him. (Is he saying *go* or *no*?) Have I just imagined that the mud is higher on his waist? His body lower in the earth? The driver's pointed teeth?

I back up slowly, then quickly, then sprint home in socked feet, screaming, frantic, bellowing for my father to come, hurry, danger, death.

The kidnapper is gone when we return. My brother is not. My father, in his trusty Timberlands, tugs my brother free.

* * *

I want to put my son at ease, to talk about his behavior. On the flip side, I don't want to make too big a deal of his sensitivities, don't want him to worry about his worry. How to calibrate this? Isn't it natural not to want to feel left out?

He had a fine day at school, he tells me afterward, followed along just fine. At home, he is back to his upbeat self, playing LEGOs with his little brother, singing a song about sharks. He takes a bath, reads to me from Frog and Toad. I pet his hair, consider the skull beneath it, the brain beneath that, how soft it is, how susceptible. I hum a lullaby. He jolts upright.

What if I can't find my classroom? he says.

What?

Parents can't go upstairs with their kids in first grade. What if I don't know where to go?

Inhale, exhale. First grade is seven months away. We'll visit ahead of time, I say. You won't get lost. Okay?

The whites of his eyes glow in the dark.

Sometimes I am jarred from sleep by the memory of being jarred from sleep. A mechanized voice explodes through the walls of my childhood bedroom. *You have violated a protected area! The police were called! Leave immediately!*

There's beeping as my father tries to disable the alarm— *Leave! Immediately!*—and concerned cries from my mother.

My father, tired, tense, presses the wrong keys, tripping a siren so loud that no one would hear me if I screamed.

Then, heart-thrumming quiet.

The creak of the stairs as he goes to investigate. The unnerving trill of the phone: a security company employee demanding a password. They need to confirm that person who picks up is not an intruder.

Probably just a malfunction, says my father, a sudden silhouette in the doorway. He is six feet tall but seems taller. Tree branch shadows slice his chest. Our alarm system is the best on the market, he reminds me. The most secure. I don't ask why we also have a motion-sensitive light at the top of the driveway and lamps attached to timers—ones whose "on" time is regularly adjusted in case anyone's noticed a pattern. I don't ask about the radios my mother switches on in the kitchen and basement whenever we leave, to give the illusion that someone's home. I don't ask why we do all this when we live in an exceptionally safe New York suburb.

Darkness whirs like static.

Go to bed, insists my father. I feel around for my stuffed bear, massage his ears into tendrils.

I wake to Oliver scream-crying. What is it? I say. What's wrong? He cannot be consoled, seems to simultaneously need me and not want me near. Does something hurt? I ask.

Don't, he says as I reach for a hug, legs and arms thrashing. Stop! His cries wake his baby brother, with whom he shares a room. The wailing doubles.

While my husband settles our toddler, I get Oliver a cup of water and a wet washcloth. I pat his forehead, which is distorted with distress.

I had a nightmare, he says finally, that you were a monster. He wants reassurance that I am who I say I am. That I'm not a demon disguised as his mom. He makes me pinkie swear. Breath snags on a branch in my throat.

It's me, I say, as our fingers interlock. It's really and only me.

Halloween 2001. In front of my Greenwich Village building, I hid in a blond wig and fur coat, my eyes charcoaled like Margot Tenenbaum's. I was twenty-three. The costume permitted me to chain-smoke.

My date for the evening: a med student I'd met at a party the week before. You shouldn't do that, he said as I lit up. He was wearing a scuba suit.

We crossed the street to the firehouse, where seven flags flapped for the Squad 18 men lost in the wreckage of the Twin Towers. We passed George W. Bush and Betty Boop and Ghostface wielding a hunting knife. Around the corner, on Greenwich Avenue, I mistook SWAT team members for costume-wearers until I saw a gym bag cordoned off by yellow tape. An officer lifted his megaphone, warned the assembling crowd to move back.

I didn't have to hear the whispers to know the word they contained. *Anthrax.* Since the cataclysm a few subway stops south, envelopes packed with the spores had been landing at news outlets and government offices around the city. Mail room employees had developed skin ulcers. Five had inhaled the bacteria and died.

Med Student tugged on my arm. We reversed our steps, scurried around the corner and past the firehouse and into my building and up to the windowless living room in my sixth-floor apartment. He was panting. In the weak lamplight, the humps of his scuba suit glowed—pectorals, crotch, knees. I imagined he'd just swum the English Channel. He shook out his hair, smoothed it aside.

I have Cipro, he said. Ciprofloxacin, the anthrax antidote. Those days, it was in short supply. He retrieved a bottle from his workbag on the floor, shook two oblong pills into his palm. Said he: Want?

At the Brooklyn nail salon, nine months pregnant with Oliver and itching for a vacation, I chose a garish purple called Bahama Mama. I needed something loud and cheery to disguise my ravaged fingernails, little landscapes I tore apart with my teeth. I was ashamed to hold out my hands.

Bad habit, I told the manicurist. She furrowed her brows. I wondered how much she understood from a person's fingers. From the stories they told. On the wall, a TV confirmed blazing spirals spinning toward New York and maps of hurricane evacuation zones, infected, red-edged scabs. She massaged my palms too hard. I did not tell her to stop.

Perhaps there was reason to panic, but I wouldn't. Even while pregnant. Especially while pregnant. From my research, I knew the risks of agitation, knew that high levels of cortisol in a stressed-out body can impair a developing fetus. This was why I was soaking my hands in warm water and why, for the past nine months, I'd attended prenatal yoga classes and received massages and tried acupuncture and paid weekly visits to a clinical psychologist and dodged interpersonal drama and violent TV. I aspired to relax.

The mental state proved harder to attain without pharmaceutical support. The social worker to whom I'd sobbed a decade prior had consulted a psychiatrist and, after trial and error and lethargy and tremors, I'd found a prescription that restored some oxygen to my lungs. Now, though, with the threat of congenital harm and chemical-laden breast milk, I'd reversed course.

In through the nose, out through the mouth: the centuries-old technique for ushering in tranquility. The air smelled of acetone.

I was seven when I lost my breath for the first time. In a house that bulged with emergency provisions (350 bottles of water, I once counted; 1,600 trash bags), I gripped the kitchen counter and wheezed until I nearly collapsed.

Dr. Horowitz had crater-covered cheeks, and while he peered down my throat, I watched a drop of sweat glide along a recessed trail, watched it pause at a crossroads near his jaw as if deciding the safest way forward.

The cold stethoscope made me hiccup. I lifted my arms, stuck out my tongue, puffed out my cheeks, pressed on his hands. Nothing appears to be wrong, he said. Still, for days afterward I struggled against shallow breaths that left me feeling wasted. I saw an allergist, whose tests proved inconclusive, and a pulmonologist, who said my condition was beyond his capacity to treat. I was suffering, he said, from hyperventilation. What I needed wasn't a medical doctor. What I needed was a shrink.

CHILDHOOD RULES

- Tape large orange reflective stickers to the front and back of your Halloween costume so cars can spot you trick-or-treating—even though you'll be teased for looking like a parking cone. (Dad: I'd rather you be a live parking cone than a dead witch!)

- Eat Halloween candy only after you've broken apart each piece to inspect it for needles and blades. Chew. Slowly.

- In the glove compartment of the car you share with your siblings, store a flashlight, a poncho, bottled water, a disposable camera, mace, and a compact emergency blanket made of Mylar, a fabric designed by NASA for space exploration.

- Do not let the fuel tank dip below half.

- Tuck the bottoms of your pants into your socks when in nature, and never, ever step barefoot in the grass. Lyme disease–carrying ticks are invisible and insidious and you could wind up like Sherry, Dad's former student: listless and allergic to light.

- Don't shower or talk on the phone during a thunderstorm; lightning can shoot through pipes or wires and fry you. *Mother Nature doesn't mess around.*

- Never wear clothes or items that display your name; a predator may try to befriend you.

- When you go on vacation, even to a nice hotel, even to a developed country, pack a suitcase full of pharmaceuticals and first-aid supplies for any potential injury or ailment.

- Lock everything, including your desk drawers, including your diary, including the small mustard-colored safe you will get for Hanukkah, including the key to said safe, which you will hide in a passcode-protected box.

The shrink had a cleft lip and low-hanging breasts and told me to call her Marlene. She supplied paper and markers and watched with folded hands as I drew.

Was it significant that I sketched the tree in my parents' backyard, the one with the toxic fruit I was warned not to eat?

Marlene pushed her oversize glasses up the bridge of her nose and followed my gaze to the Xerox machine. Did I want to make copies? I nodded, and presto! A dozen sets of sinewy branch-arms and elliptical leaves and patches of grass strewn with rotten apples. I taped a few to her wood-paneled walls, then moved on to the hallway. Up went tree after tree, a protective row, at the end of which was the waiting area—and my parents. Their expressions were cryptic and unstable, mouths alternating between semi-smiles and half frowns.

Having fun? they said.

I visited Marlene a few more times. At our last session, I took her picture with my lavender camera, just as I took pictures of my oatmeal and my comb, just as I used a diary to catalog my playdates and the books I checked out of the library. When my mom offered to take a photo of Marlene and me, we shuffled together. In the image, I look cheery, my braid brushing the high waistband of her skirt, the teeth in my mouth at various stages of coming and going. I still believed in the tooth fairy. Was the source of my stress just as mythical? What did I say was plaguing me?

Maybe the signs were hard to read. Maybe Marlene missed them. All I know is that my treatment concluded. My disquiet did not.

* * *

I browse medical journals and textbooks to learn about parent-child transfer. I find articles on neurobiology and heredity and the hypothalamic-pituitary-adrenal axis. I read about uniparental inheritance, how the maternal passing-on of mitochondria means children carry more of their mother's genes than their father's. I read a study about six hundred rhesus monkeys from a multigenerational family, and how the primates with anxious temperaments ceased to move or coo in the presence of a "potentially threatening human intruder" while their even-tempered relatives didn't react. The study is unnerving. The text is dense, inscrutable. I ask my therapist for interpretive help. She finds the study unnerving. She finds the text dense, inscrutable. She wants to know what I'm looking for.

Evidence, I say.

Of what?

Anxiety migrated and morphed in adolescence, usually unprovoked. A shadow that appeared and retreated depending on the position of the sun, stalking my body but separate from it. It showed itself in the cuticles I pecked and picked at until they oozed and throbbed. At age eleven, it settled in my jaw, which ceased to be able to chew more than a few bites without burning. TMJ disorder resulted from clenching my teeth like fists. The dentist outfitted me with a clear plastic mouth guard that I had to wear day and night for a year and scrub with a toothbrush. Worry even crept into my capillaries, causing my nose to bleed while reading, while running, while taking exams. Sorry, I told teachers as I submitted answer sheets festooned with pink, feathery smears. Droplets I'd tried to efface with my sleeve. At fifteen, I got cauterized, a procedure during which an ENT stuck up my nose a wand that emitted an electric current to singe and seal the vessels. Still, it bled.

I turn the dial, try a different combination, wait for a click.

The elementary school social worker is an overworked, patient brunette who writes Oliver's name on the lip of a file folder. When I describe his behavior, she proposes observing him in class.

I want to see his environment, she says.

His environment. I can speak to it, too, if she wants to know. I can tell her that we have no alarm system or emergency provisions. That he doesn't wear reflective stickers on Halloween and that he carries a backpack that bears his name. I can speak to his uterine environment too. The measures I took. The yoga. And yet.

How do you respond when he gets anxious? she asks.

Well, I say, I don't want to exacerbate it, so I speak in a soft and measured way. I put up a shield of faux calm.

She nods, jots something down on a scrap of paper, slides it across the table. It's a doctor in Park Slope, she says. Maybe if you talk to her you can respond to him with real calm instead of faux calm.

There is a crab apple in my throat. I understand the connotation. I am grateful she does not say it aloud. In this equation, I am both his nature and his nurture.

*   *   *

Your breath: Diaphragm flattens, ribs rise, oxygen tunnels through tubes, and air sacs fill, lungs inflate. And the reverse: rise, fall, deflate.

I had my first panic attack in college, in a fine arts building bathroom, on a break from Drawing II. I held the stall walls as my breath thrashed and the world galloped and the tiles trembled under my feet. I sweated through a pair of overalls. My teeth chattered all the way home.

Shortly after graduation, overwhelmed with being over-whelmed, I looked up *therapist* in the yellow pages and selected whomever in my vicinity could meet the soonest. My would-be savior was a pale, plump, soft-spoken social worker in Green-wich Village. She had barely taken off her coat when I collapsed in sobs.

Here's what I told my date on Halloween in 2001 when I declined his Cipro: If we were going the way of biological warfare, if the apocalypse were imminent, I didn't want to be left on a planet populated exclusively by neurotics with survival kits. I would rather die.

An attempted abduction at our local playground. I alert my husband, text the babysitter, set my jaw. That night, I tell my children about stranger danger. What if someone approaches you and says they're Mommy's friend? I ask. What if someone acts like they know you? They are the same questions my parents used to ask me, the same scenarios. I tell my children, as my parents told me: Always check with your grown-up.

At the nail salon, a message from my mother: Fill your bathtub with water!

Moments later, from my father: Pack a go bag with your important papers!

My parents no longer speak—divorce—but their voices unite in crises. Hurricane Irene registered as a Category 4. Storms this intense, said the meteorologist, could produce winds of 150 miles per hour. A cartoon cloud appeared on the screen with puffed-out cheeks and vexed brows, lines of air tunneling from its mouth. Out the window, locals rolled suitcases down the sidewalk and joined a queue snaking out of the supermarket, where bottled water was already in short supply.

At home that night, while the wind picked up and the lights quivered, while my husband gathered candles and flashlights, I sang a song to my belly. *Goodnight, Irene. Goodnight, Irene. I'll see you in my dreams.* I sang and I hummed, unaware of the rest of the lyrics. *Sometimes I live in the country. Sometimes I live in town. Sometimes I have a great notion to jump into the river and drown.*

By 2 a.m., our windows clattered and Oliver twisted and kicked. Not tonight, I whispered. Hang on. Taxis had stopped running. The local hospital had cleared out its patients and bolted its doors after a generator lost power. I wondered if I should've taken protective measures. If my nonchalance would compromise my family's safety. Only later would I learn that the New York City Emergency Management department recommended that residents prepare a go bag with small bills and identifying documents in waterproof sleeves, that it advised having an emergency supply kit stocked for survival for seven days, complete with a gallon of drinking water per person per day, nonperishable foods, a wind-up radio, and iodine pills. I would discover that some people in my social circle took such precautions. A friend who keeps headlamps and an air horn at the ready. Another, harnesses and a belaying device. I'd learn about a distant cousin's store of tampons to plug "a gash, deep cut, bullet wound, or some other serious puncture." I'd long assumed such measures created an illusion of control in the face of upheaval. Like my parents' glove compartment stash. When, in 2020, a coronavirus would require us to quarantine for countless months, and we'd all wear masks and gloves and avoid people and stores would run out of everything, I would wonder who the wise ones were. How impossible it had been to imagine a crisis of such magnitude, one that would require measures so extreme. How easy it had been to roll my eyes.

Out the bedroom window, branches waved like drowning arms. I rubbed the bump of Oliver's heel and picked Bahama Mama off my nails until my claws peeked through.

In the morning I strolled still streets, past a felled branch, an upturned umbrella. I paced the promenade, pressed against the railing, and squinted across New York Harbor at the cranes looming over Ground Zero.

Oliver can't breathe. These are the words he uses. His younger brother has asthma, and he wants to know if he needs medicine too. If he needs a nebulizer. If he'll need an inhaler. I watch his shoulders rise, eyes widen, chest swell. He can't breathe in all the way, he says, can't take a deep breath. It's not like wheezing. It's different.

I stare agog. Think about something else, I say, something peaceful. Picture the beach. It's a cliché that never helped me, but in the moment, I strain to remember what did. I am too horrified that there might be a kink in human DNA that maps not just to childhood anxiety but to this precise presentation of it.

On a train from New York to New Jersey, I yawn and recall a time my mother tried to reverse a bout of childhood insomnia. Focus on one limb of your body at a time, she whispered in the dark. Tell each toe to relax.

The train squeaks to a halt in Newark, but the doors in our car fail to open. A woman out of sight begins to shout, Where do I get out?

Then there's my father, flexing his biceps to quell concern that someone might climb through my bedroom window, impossibly hard orbs that my hands cannot encircle. Who would mess with this? he says. Who?

The woman on the train is getting louder, more frantic. Someone, tell me where to get out! No one responds; no one knows. I look around for an employee. I don't see one.

Neither of my parents remembers me being so anxious. My memories surprise them. Confuse them. *Are you sure?*

The following week, I will teach my son to practice blowing soap bubbles through a plastic wand, a technique to summon calm that I'll read about online. Take a deep breath so you can make a big bubble, I'll explain, but blow out slowly so the bubble doesn't pop. He will watch me do it and he will learn and we will regain control.

Help, the woman shouts. Her voice is almighty. I need to get off! The train has already begun to roll.

HOT FOR TEACHER

WHAT DID THEY WANT? More than anything? Violent things. Unattainable things.

More than anything, she wanted to taste blood, said one student.

More than anything, he wanted freedom, said another.

Your characters need to have desires, I'd explained in the previous class. Drama arises when people struggle to get what they want.

Their first writing assignment of the semester at this public East Coast college: compose a short fictional sketch that begins with wanting. Compelling, complex fiction, I'd said, grows out of desires great and small. Their opening sentences offered proof:

More than anything, she wanted a baby.

More than anything, he wanted things to return to the way they were.

Then we arrived at Charlie in the back row, a pale, acne-pocked sophomore who rarely participated in class discussions. I'd surmised he was shy, but it was early in the term. I was making assumptions.

More than anything, Charlie read in an even voice, he wanted for her to realize that she shouldn't depend on the bankers or lawyers he imagined she dated, that it wasn't them who could really and truly satisfy her, but it was him—a student in her Tuesday writing class—who could and would push aside the pile of ungraded papers and take her passionately atop her desk, him with whom she belonged in a way that only the romantic poetry she taught them could convey.

Twenty pairs of eyes pinned me in place. I willed my face not to blush, my voice not to crack.

Okay, I said, just as I had to the student who'd shared work before him.

More than anything, I wanted to scream expletives in his face.

Charlie's expression was inscrutable; he seemed neither proud nor nervous. Perhaps a little expectant, like he'd just ordered takeout and was waiting to be told how much it cost. That passage, I said, has a nice rhythm to it, a nice cadence. I leaned back against the table, my rear precariously close to the pile of ungraded papers. I would not let him have his way with me. The repetition, I said, is poetic.

The repetition, I wanted to say, *keeps your voice loud while mine is silent.*

I moved on to the student next to him, one whose character, more than anything, wanted a piece of pie.

It is February in Brooklyn and the café speakers try to counteract the cold. They blast Southern soul in the form of Joe Tex's "I Gotcha," a song I know from the film *Reservoir Dogs*. I understand the story in its lyrics. It was mine one Friday night in high school, when I left a friend's basement to use the upstairs bathroom. The second floor was dark, the house asleep, but I knew the way. When I emerged from the bathroom into the shadowy hallway, her older brother's friend was waiting—for the toilet, I assumed. I recognized his football jersey and backward baseball cap, but not the thin-lipped smile he put inches from my face, or the pressure of his bony hands on my hips, or the way he moved his body from side to side with mine as I tried to dodge him. The entrapment dance. When I retreated backward, he stepped forward, until my heel hit the tile at the entrance to the bathroom. He was going to push me in there, I realized. He was going to push me onto the cold floor and lock the door behind him and everyone was in the basement and nobody would hear me scream. I tasted iron in the back of my throat, a bloody nose, belted, *Let me through!* and somehow wriggled past.

But we're not talking about a dance; we're talking about a song. A groovy, horn-filled tune whose lyrics describe how a man, more than anything, wants a woman against her will.

Now kiss me.

Hold it a long time. Hold it.

Don't turn it a-loose, now. Hold it.

My first-ever intimate encounter was an unwelcome kiss. I was nine. Todd had advertised his crush on me, told classmates I had a *nice ass*, crude language that made me giggle. Was I supposed to feel flattered? Stung? (Todd would later try to retract the comment, slipping a sheet of yellow paper into the cave of my school desk, a letter I inexplicably saved: "I'm sorry for what I said. You do have a nice ass, but only in jeans.")

One afternoon in the park, Todd announced that he wanted a kiss. *Your characters need to have desires.* I didn't want to kiss him, nor did I want to be kissed, but the more I refused, the more he insisted, until a chase ensued. Just a kiss, he called. I sprinted and screamed, No! Everyone laughed and cheered him on, including my girlfriends. Terror bloomed in my blood. *Drama arises when people struggle to get what they want.* I wound up curled facedown in the dirt, hands and arms blocking the sides of my face, heart hammering.

What was I afraid of? I couldn't have told you then, but I can tell you now. I was afraid of how words we both understood—*Leave me alone!*—suddenly had no effect. Of how my body didn't belong to me alone.

Todd found a sliver of exposed skin between my earlobe and neck and crushed his lips against it.

* * *

I was twenty-nine in that East Coast classroom, young for an academic but I was not a newbie. I'd already taught hundreds of students, and several challenging ones. I had practiced diverting attention from in-class disruptions and channeling excitement into animated discussions. Still, I couldn't determine what Charlie wanted. To see me squirm? Flush? Freak out? I broke the class into groups to complete a collaborative exercise. Did he expect a sultry invitation to office hours? Or was this his idea of a joke? A performance for classmates? A way to shove the teacher while everyone watched to see if she'd wobble, then fall?

In high school, I became the fixation of a foreign-exchange student. Farouk not only memorized my schedule but seemed to know its digressions. If I showed up early to work in the painting studio, Farouk would find me and try to make small talk, apologizing for his poor English. He attended my sports matches, once lingered outside my math class—a bodiless face framed in the door's small window. I laughed off his overtures, poked fun at them with friends. I thought that ignoring him would translate my lack of interest and hamper his, but he only redoubled his efforts. He sent gifts to my house and oversize cards featuring black-and-white stock photos of a little boy and girl. In one, they sat on a stoop, his lips pressed to her cheek, her long-lashed eyes circular and open wide. I was his perfect girl, he wrote, amid blobs of Wite-Out. Couldn't he be my friend?

Most of Farouk's packages included self-addressed stamped envelopes to facilitate a reply, which he never received.

I didn't seek formal intervention, because his advances, while excessive, didn't seem threatening to my school-age self. Not even when his senior yearbook quote, below his headshot, included a proclamation that he'd always love me, as well as a national farewell: "See ya, USA!"

Then there's the doctor whom I saw from pubescence through my early twenties. An obstetrician. He treated my mother too. Doctor gave me breast exams with clammy pink hands, an activity whose awkwardness he tried to override with chatter. Where was I applying to college? Did I know what I wanted to study? It was good that I liked to read, he said, because we might be snowed in over the weekend. Had I heard about the forecasted storm? He was thorough with the palpating, he said, because I had dense breasts. Up close the hairs of his white mustache and beard were thicker than I'd expected, his forehead more mottled. His wedding band felt smooth against my skin.

Doctor was the first man to touch me. He gave me exhaustive pelvic exams during which he asked questions about my sexual habits and told me that due to the structure of my anatomy, intercourse in certain positions would be uncomfortable. He tilted his head, which was framed between my knees, asking if this was the case. Was it? Uncomfortable?

A year or so later, in a crowded rock club, someone slipped a hand up my skirt and their fingers inside me. I shrieked and spun around, but the bass overwhelmed my voice and in the low light there was only a lattice of flesh, lips, and hands shifting and slithering—one mighty, insidious beast.

Should I have done more to protect myself? Even as a grown woman, I was steeped in self-doubt. By the end of my class with Charlie, I'd determined I needed to be more objective. This was a creative writing class, one in which we read stories across the inflammatory spectrum. Maybe I was overreacting. Maybe I'd misremembered the specificity of the student's writing or its intensity—dismissive tendencies that, I see now, encourage rapacious behavior.

I located his assignment on the train home and discovered, in sentence two, that his character favored his professor's striped sweater dress—something I'd worn to our last class—which highlighted her pendulous breasts. The next page offered similar drivel. I slammed my folder closed.

* * *

College: a middle-of-the-night phone call from a guy who said he had gotten my name from a mutual friend. The caller thought I was pretty "in a natural way." He hoped we could talk. When, in a sleepy daze, I pressed him—Which friend again?—the line went dead. I dismissed the exchange as a prank, until he called a few nights later, and again the night after that. Each time, I slammed down the phone and only half remembered the occurrence the following morning. When, on his fifth or sixth call, he complimented my cute blue row house, I called the police. The officers had neither a number nor a name to trace—this was the year 2000—so other than showing up in the morning's wee hours to record my complaint, they could only offer words:

Be vigilant. Be careful. Let us know if there's any more activity.

There was plenty of activity—for an agitated imagination. For weeks, I eyeballed every lone male in my path, analyzed every noise outside my window, and jogged to and from evening classes with keys laced between my fingers. I struggled to sleep. Feared my ringing phone, and feared unplugging it too.

Maybe the caller was a neighbor. Maybe he had been peering out his window when the squad car pulled up and watched me welcome officers into my cute blue row house, face warped with worry. Maybe he realized he'd gone too far. Or didn't want to get caught. He never called again.

*   *   *

Was it? Uncomfortable? What was uncomfortable was Doctor's question, which I assumed was par for the course in a gynecological exam. After all, I was paying a stranger to handle and inquire about my private parts. Sometimes, in his office, I'd stare at the framed photos of his blond children to feel more at ease.

When precancerous cells were discovered on my cervix, Doctor performed the excision. I was twenty-six. My mother accompanied me, and I squeezed her hand while he peered between my legs and spread numbing gel on my cervix and used a hot electrical wire to cut away the abnormal tissue. Afterward, I cramped and bled.

A few months later, I returned to graduate school in Tucson, where I found a new doctor.

My boyfriend, neither a lawyer nor a banker, as Charlie assumed, was outraged. The kid sounds psychotic, he said. You shouldn't go back to class.

That's absurd, I replied, unwilling to cower. Of course, the thought had occurred to me too. This was months after the Virginia Tech massacre, wherein a male undergrad killed thirty-two people, the deadliest mass shooting on a college campus to date. The gunman had intimidated girls in his poetry class by taking pictures of their legs. Which is not to say I thought Charlie was plotting murder. I just couldn't read his behavior.

Neither could the English Department chair, to whom

I forwarded his assignment. She was apprehensive when she called him in for a one-on-one meeting the following day, joking to me that if the worst-case scenario came to pass, I could have her back issues of the *Paris Review*. Charlie, meanwhile, was baffled—or wore that mask. In his writing assignment, he'd not only changed the day our class met, he told her, but also changed the color of my hair! As he seemed neither hostile nor deranged, and since he apologized, his sentence was to be removed from the class and commence an independent study with a male professor.

For the rest of the term, I considered how it hadn't mattered that I had ten years on Charlie and more degrees, or that I could have failed him with the stroke of a pen. He'd still felt compelled to exert sexual power. I was still a woman.

It's a catchy tune that's filling up the café. Customers tap their feet and hum.

> *You made me a promise and you're gonna stick to it.*
> *You shouldn't have promised if you weren't gonna do it.*

Survey the crowd. There are familiar faces there, including my sons, ages four and six. They like the song too. Bop their heads. Lick whipped cream off hot chocolate.

> *You saw me and ran in another direction.*
> *I'll teach you to play with my affections.*

Later, when I hear my boys singing the chorus—*Give it here!*—
I can explain that I dislike its message, that a man's *yes* is never
more powerful than a woman's *no*. I can parlay this into the
"Respect People's Bodies" talk that some teachers have advised
parents to give. *You shouldn't touch another person, and no person
should touch you, without permission*, I can say. *Ask before you hug
someone. Assert "No thank you" to the offer of a hug if you're not in
the mood. Same with holding hands: ask or give permission.*

I can teach them about sexism, too, and point to ines-
capable indoctrinations: the Mrs. and Miss titles they use
alongside the singular Mr.; the male faces emblazoned on the
coins in their piggybanks; the boy toys endorsing confronta-
tional play. I can explain how inequality begets bias begets
discrimination begets intimidation begets assault. How if
they see anyone forcing a kiss upon someone, they should
intervene. That allowing such behavior not only implicates
them, but permits another act that's one degree more heinous,
and makes witnesses one degree more tolerant, until there's
no shame in grabbing a woman by the pussy, until sixty-two
million Americans say *yes* to a presidential candidate who
brags about doing just that.

I can model good behavior, too, can take aside that boy on
the playground who's pulling a girl's hair while she squeals.

Let's not do that, I tell him. She's letting you know she
doesn't like it.

The girl sniffles. The boy takes off.

Watch my sons watch me. It's good to be a helper, I say.

* * *

In 2015, a suit filed in the New York Supreme Court in Manhattan detailed Doctor's rampant sexual abuse, including how he vaginally and anally probed female patients with gloveless fingers. Nineteen women described behavior dating back to the early 1990s; that number would quadruple after presidential candidate Andrew Yang's wife, Evelyn, spoke out against Doctor in 2019. Evelyn had been pregnant at the time of the assault, as had others. Two victims were in high school. Oftentimes, Doctor would examine women with a nurse present and then return after the nurse left, claiming he forgot to check something. At trial, he admitted to forcible touching to gratify his sexual desire and to engaging in "sexual conduct against a patient for no valid medical purpose while she was incapable of consent."[1] More than one woman had felt his tongue between her legs.

Due to the criminal statute of limitations for most of the victims, and Doctor's fierce defense team, which worked to discredit his accusers, Doctor landed a handsome deal. He pled guilty to a single low-level felony and one misdemeanor, and instead of going to jail or being put on probation, he surrendered his medical license. Moreover, since the Manhattan DA agreed to downgrade Doctor's sex offender status to the lowest level, he doesn't even appear on the sex offender registry.[2]

* * *

Summer 2018. I am a faculty member at a writing program in Greece. I bring along my family, and my four-year-old, Leo, strikes up a friendship with a local girl named Ivana. For days, they are inseparable, playing tag, trading bites of ice cream, searching for stray cats. One evening, while they pose for photos at an adult's behest, someone shouts, Kiss her, Leo! A chorus erupts: Kiss her! Kiss her! Leo leans over, holds his pucker to Ivana's face while camera flashes flicker.

I could've interceded. Said to the chorus, *Why don't they just smile?* But there is live music and dancing and everyone is merry and I don't want to be a killjoy. It is over in seconds.

Ivana seems unbothered. After she leaves to play, a friend shows me his camera snapshot. In it, Leo's eyes are shut tight, Ivana's wide open.

HOLY BODY

THE INSTRUCTIONS, FRAMED ON the sink, are more thorough and explicit than you'd expect. USE THE TISSUES TO EMPTY YOUR NOSE AND THE TOILET TO EMPTY YOUR BLADDER, they say. USE THE SHOWER TO LATHER AND RINSE EVERY LIMB AND STRAND: EARS, ELBOWS, GENITALS, TOES.

There are supplies. Q-tips and cotton rounds. Toothpaste, a toothbrush, floss, a comb. There is nail polish remover to de-lacquer fingernails and toenails and cleanser to clear away makeup and a pumice stone to slough dead skin off your heels. There is a dish for the items you're asked to remove: eyeglasses, wedding bands, dental plates, hearing aids.

THERE SHOULD BE NO PHYSICAL BARRIERS BETWEEN THE BODY AND THE LIVING WATERS. YOU SHOULD BE AS NAKED AS ON THE DAY OF YOUR BIRTH.

There are also meditations. Seven of them.

Seven. The number of steps you will soon descend into the water. The figure represents wholeness and the creative process, according to the text framed on the sink: God—and this is a house of God—took six days to create the world but made his work complete on the seventh, the Sabbath, a day of rest. You are dubious about God but believe in completion and the creative process. You are, for example, writing a book you hope to finish.

Both physical and spiritual directives have the same aim: to cleanse and prime and hone your focus. The suite in which you stand has also been occupied by the dying and the barely survived. By the grieving. By the newly married and the freshly divorced. By the abused and the barren. By those who are mid-transformation and the transformed. By the reverent. By a woman who went blind in midlife—a fate you cannot fathom—and a paraplegic whose wife is expecting twins.

IN THE MIKVEH, EVERY BODY IS A SACRED VESSEL.

You may hear echoes of these folks as you undress, see shadows behind folds of the shower curtain, flashes in the mirror. You may wonder about the words they held in their mouths when they stood where you are. Try, though, to concentrate on your own words, on your own mouth. Heed the meditations.

1. *HINEINI.*
HERE I AM.

You are here because of Carrie, who works upstairs at the mikveh center, and whom you haven't seen in a dozen years.

You met Carrie nearly three decades ago, at age ten, at a Jewish sleepaway camp in the Berkshires. You would share a cabin for seven consecutive summers, fourteen months in all. But that first day, you knew no one save your older sister, in a distant bunk. You and Carrie were in the camp's youngest unit, Bonim, Hebrew for "builders." For the first few days, you wondered what you would be asked to build.

It is hard to remember the order of things. Did you gravitate to each other because you looked alike, or did a friendship sprout from counselors pointing out a resemblance? Maybe looks had nothing to do with it. Maybe you made each other laugh. Or had a mutually satisfying stationery trade: your denim-print envelopes for her hot-pink ones. You do remember how, the following June, you told Carrie the story of your friend from home who'd been killed by a car in the intervening year. She remembers too—how you showed her pictures, black-and-whites from a small album you kept under your pillow. That friend had been an identical twin. Did you want a twin too? You and Carrie didn't look identical, but you did have the same un-crimpably straight brown hair and dark eyes and pale skin and full cheeks. You were the same height. And your names—Carrie, Courtney, with their consonantal starts and openmouthed middles and merry ends—resembled each other when spoken quickly, which is the only way one spoke at camp.

One Friday night, you wore matching flowy, floral dresses and styled your hair the same way so you could screw with people in the dining hall. Nobody fell for your shtick, not really, but you liked thinking they had. In fact, when you showed your husband a camp photo of the two of you from 1990, he thought, for a second, that preteen her was preteen you.

You and Carrie saw each other a handful of times after you outgrew camp. She returned for a few summers as a counselor. You, instead, got a job folding clothes at your local mall. In college, she studied social work and developed an academic interest in Judaism that led her to become observant—somewhere, you gather, between Conservative and modern Orthodox, though she eschews labels. She met a boy who was on the same track; they married and moved to Israel, studied at a yeshiva, and eventually settled outside of Boston. They have three children, all of whom have Hebrew names. At night before bed, Carrie sings these words from the Torah to her children: *Shema Yisrael: Adonai eloheinu, Adonai echad.* Hear, O Israel: the Lord is our God, the Lord is One.

You studied literature and art in college and grew skeptical of everything, including, and maybe especially, organized religion. You became a writer and went to graduate school and married an agnostic musician from a devout Baptist family. Together, you have two sons whose names have no Hebrew equivalent. You forewent their brises, opting for hospital circumcisions instead, because you find the public nature of the practice disconcerting and you didn't want to cement your children's eternal covenant with the Lord, the ritual's intent. Still, because you are Jewishly inclined, you had a baby-naming ceremony for your firstborn at a progressive Brooklyn synagogue, where the rabbi played acoustic guitar and everyone, especially you, clapped along. The songs were the same ones you sang at camp. Your sons eat latkes on Hanukkah and pot roast on Christmas and matzo on Passover and Peeps on Easter (your mother-in-law sends a basket in the mail). You do too. On weekdays you teach English at a United Methodist–affiliated liberal arts college, whose church archives are among the most comprehensive in the world. Your relationship to Judaism is addled, inconsistent.

Hineini. Here I am. Abraham's reply when God asks him to tie up his son Isaac and slit his throat. A blind faith of which you feel incapable—or unwilling to adhere to. The kind of faith small children place in their parents.

To wit: When your husband was five, his dad signed him up to play Son to his Father in a church production. At rehearsal, under a priest's direction, they marched through the sanctuary and across the stage and paused in front of a giant cross, where your father-in-law raised his hands above his head. Your husband was puzzled, but he was five and often puzzled by adult behavior. The night of the performance, your husband received a toga to wear and a bundle of sticks to carry. His father received a knife. Your husband felt inexplicable panic.

Why do you have that? he asked.

It's just a prop, said his father.

To use on me?

His father laughed, said, No, no, of course not.

Moments later, they repeated what they'd rehearsed, your husband walking through the sanctuary, now full of congregants, and across the stage, stopping in front of the giant cross, where his father once again raised his hands, this time a blade in his grip. You can imagine the dark, exaggerated shadow on the stage floor, the knife stretched into a sword, his father's face a blackish blot, absent features and expression. You can imagine that the spotlights blinded him, prevented him from seeing his mother in the pews. Your husband says he peeked over his shoulder just as his father dropped the weapon. He can still summon the relief he felt when he arrived at the other side of the stage unharmed—probably not unlike Isaac, whom Abraham, with God's permission, released unharmed.

What's the lesson? That you should love your creator more than you do your kids? That blind faith will protect you?

Hineini. You are here, in Massachusetts, getting naked in the bathroom of this religious center because of Carrie, but also because of another kind of faith: Pregnancy. Parenthood. Carrie is serving as a gestational surrogate. Which is to say, she is several months pregnant with another couple's baby.

It is unthinkable to you, her willingness to go through the consuming, intimate, intense process of pregnancy and delivery for total strangers, for a child that isn't hers. Surrogacy seems more like a hypothetical scenario you'd broach over dinner with friends, only to declare it too taxing, too invasive, too involved. But Carrie has made this abstraction real. Carrie, whose announcement about surrogacy on social media left you stunned, whose regular updates and insights on her experience you have ravenously consumed, whose photos of sonograms— her womb, someone else's fetus—you have invariably "liked," even if the thumbs-up is more an indication of awe.

Also, of envy—not because she became a surrogate and you didn't, but because she's the kind of person who would. Who did. You want to be a model of generosity and kindness for your children, have told your husband you think this is most important— more than intelligence or industriousness or creativity, qualities that your well-to-do Brooklyn enclave esteems, qualities that seemed most valued in your hometown too. Good grades and scored goals earn bragging rights and bumper stickers. Less so, empathy. Your parents and teachers and camp counselors taught you to be kind, but, like everyone, you got mixed messages.

Consider: In fourth grade, after reading Roald Dahl's *George's Marvelous Medicine*, you made an illustrated book lampooning your great-aunt, your grandpa's sister, a small, chain-smoking spinster with wild eyes whom you saw on Jewish holidays. You remember sketching her curved spine, pressing a yellow crayon into each square tooth, contriving metaphors for her carcinogenic stench. You remember, too, how hard your family laughed when you showed them your creation, how your mom displayed it on the kitchen windowsill, which filled you with pride. Years later your aunt would die alone in her Manhattan apartment, would be discovered when the fumes of her rotting corpse seeped under the doors of her neighbors. Your grandfather would chastise the crowd at her burial, his voice rubbed raw: This is all of our faults.

Your great-aunt had knit you a cardigan sweater that you kept in your closet long after you outgrew it. Eyeing the thick wool, the sunburst of pink and purple on the shoulders, the ornate silver buttons, evoked so much in you—the cruel book, the cruel death. Sometimes you turned on your closet light just to stare at it. Sometimes you gripped its scratchy wrist.

As a new mother, you were sensitive to a world saturated with vitriol and rancor. To how intolerant politicians stoked ire. You wanted to cultivate humans whose behavior offset this or called it out, aspired to be a model of compassion for your children. And yet Carrie's generosity delineated the limits of your own. How had she become so empathic?

You sent her an email, wished her mazel tov on the pregnancy. You were impressed, you said—more than that, astonished. You didn't add that pregnancy was something you had no interest in doing again for your own family, let alone for someone else's. Nor did you say that your husband had just had a vasectomy, which you encouraged. The procedure placed an exclamation point after the size of both your biological family and your uterus, a realization you didn't process until later.

Carrie was pleased to hear from you, called you Courtez, a camp nickname. You had questions about her surrogacy and her life, you said; you were eager to catch up. Was she free in the coming weeks? You could hop on the train to Boston.

Anything for you, she said. You resisted the urge to ask if

she'd carry your next of kin. She had a guest room where you could crash, she said. Also, she wrote, "ice cream in the freezer and three small kids you can feel free to yell at anytime if you want that home-away-from-home feel." And in an instant, you remembered why you'd become friends.

2. *HIDDUR MITZVAH*. THE UNADORNED BODY IS BEAUTIFUL IN ITSELF.

In the preparation suite, you do as you are told: "Take a few moments to really look at yourself in the mirror." You consider your nakedness, the padding on your hips, the slight sag in your breasts. *Hiddur mitzvah*.

You have never taken a ritual bath. You thought the experience was only for Orthodox Jewish women needing a post-menstrual cleanse, or a concluding ritual for converts. But this mikveh center has an unconventional mission: to help Jews of all stripes honor life transitions or commemorate occasions. It is novel for a mikveh to be so accessible, even to nonbelievers. The idea of slowing down, looking closely, appeals to your overworked sensibilities. Also appealing: understanding Carrie by immersing in her lifework.

You'd spotted her easily on the Route 128 station platform the day before, she whose belly protruded from behind a post. You still have the same-color hair, but hers is cut shorter. And you're now 5'8" to her 5'7". In her SUV, she pointed out that it was probably the first time you'd ridden in a car together. It was true; campers don't drive.

Congrats on getting your license, you said. Her laugh was quick and familiar. You wanted to stare at this childhood friend all grown-up, to see what was the same and what was different, but in a matter of seconds the woman effaced the girl.

Your catch-up starts even before you pull out of the parking lot and unfolds along the highway and at an outdoor café and over dinner at a sports bar and in the living room of her spacious suburban house and eventually migrates into the backyard, where she tends to a coop of pecking chickens while you contemplate their eggs.

Carrie tells you that, pre-surrogacy, she would brag about how good she was at bringing babies into the world, how she should just keep doing this thing she was good at doing. She had conceived each of her kids—now ten, seven, and four—on the first try and had relished pregnancy. It felt good. She felt good. Her gestations were uncomplicated, as were her births. She'd never had a miscarriage, never had to terminate. She hadn't suffered postpartum depression. Never puked. She delivered all of her babies vaginally, in the hospital, without epidural anesthesia. The longest of any of her births, from first contraction to audible newborn cry, was four hours. None of her children emerged with serious medical conditions or complications.

This is how Carrie first explains the desirability of surrogacy. Her pregnancy skills. Her success rate. Also, she says, I get to eat all the sweets I want. And I look cute with a belly. It's like getting to wear a cool accessory. This is the Carrie in whom you recognize yourself: the sarcasm, the deadpan delivery.

Hiddur mitzvah. The unadorned body is beautiful in itself?

You got pregnant quickly too. You had a pelvic condition while carrying your firstborn, but only in the last trimester, and it dissipated upon his birth, a C-section. Your second pregnancy was relatively problem-free and your son was born vaginally and quickly. You liked being pregnant too—the marvel of it, the sensation of somersaults under your skin. Still, it wouldn't have occurred to you to do what Carrie's doing and, even if it had, you would never have researched it. And were you to look into it, just for kicks, and learn that it was possible, even at your age, and that there were desperate folks you could help, you would never pursue it.

Is it relevant that you have the organ donor box checked on your driver's license, putting your anatomy up for grabs after you pass? You have no problem with someone wearing your eyeballs when you no longer need them. But Carrie is offering up herself while she is very much alive, while she needs her body to walk and work and have sex with her husband and chase after her children.

You ask more questions, dig deeper, learn about her mother, a redhead whose face you haven't pictured in twenty-five years and who likely doesn't look like she did on visiting day in 1992.

Her mother, who gave Carrie five dollars in singles to distribute to the down-and-out on each visit to New York City. Her mother, who encouraged Carrie to include on her bat mitzvah invitation an atypical request to guests: Please bring canned food, clothes, or toys to the service. *I would like to share my special day with those less fortunate*, Carrie told invitees, you included, in glossy pink print. *Helping others*, she wrote, *will really make the day complete*. Her mother, who maintains there is always a way to improve someone else's situation.

Pleasurable pregnancies. A magnanimous parent. Also, Carrie says, camp.

Indeed, there were lackluster educational activities every summer. Mornings when a charismatic rabbi led discussions of moral lessons from the Torah, though you can't recall what they were. An afternoon spent frowning at the environmental effects of pollution. An evening when you navigated a room blindfolded so you could relate to the visually impaired. It's hard to disentangle the knowledge you acquired at camp from what you learned at school and from books and from your parents. Everything blends. You have more lucid summer memories of sneaking out with friends in the middle of the night, sprinting under a star-studded sky to boys' camp. Of shaving your legs on a grassy hill in the rain. Of getting your period one summer session and thinking not about fertility or mikvehs or family planning but about how to use a tampon, advice a friend (Carrie?) offered through a bathroom stall door. Of a bedtime serenade your cabin received from a male song leader, who, in lieu of singing, described his experience administering oral sex. Camp.

Carrie doesn't remember that lewd confession, though she does recall a female counselor demonstrating how to give a hand job on a broomstick. Clearly, carnal conversation made an impression on both of you. Why not, then, the ethical how-tos? Why did they influence her in more meaningful ways? Were you that distractible? Hormonal? Uninterested?

Carrie wants to do something irrefutably good, she says between sips of decaf. The kind of thing she can point to whenever she questions her self-worth and feel reassured. Yes, she runs a nonprofit in whose mission she believes—it helps people cope and heal and deepen their spiritual connection—but she strategizes and fundraises more than she interacts with visitors. Sometimes it's hard to see impact. To feel fulfilled. Carrie is buoyed by concrete outcomes. Like a belly. Like a baby.

Her tone is matter-of-fact, but the logic doesn't convince you. There are plenty of ways to do palpable good.

Why not donate a kidney? you say. Your smile is coy, but your question is serious. Why *not*? You don't add that this is something you probably wouldn't do, either, especially for a stranger. Even though an estimated twelve people die daily because they haven't received this imperative transplant. Even though scientists are looking into pig organs, since human supply falls so short of demand. You are surprised by her disinclination—No interest, she says, pupils darting to her lap and back up again—and she's not a registered organ donor. You are surprised, and maybe a bit relieved, to discover that her net of radical empathy doesn't stretch over everything, as you'd assumed. This is about creating life, not saving it.

Pregnancy feels important, she says. It feels meaningful.

Someone else might find meaning in supplying bone marrow or a lung—both options for living donors. Also eligible: donating part of the pancreas or one of the two lobes of your liver, since livers regenerate. You have looked into this while ruminating on her surrogacy. Healthy humans have several parts that can save or improve others' lives. You are dismayed by the knowledge that you are not one of these self-sacrificing humans.

Carrie thinks that people want their generosity to have a limited personal impact. Nobody wants to get their hands dirty, in other words. Or their uteri. It's far easier and cleaner to make a donation. Or call a congressman. Or write an essay.

She doesn't understand this feeling. She doesn't understand why she's never met another surrogate. She doesn't understand why you haven't either.

3. NEKAVIM NEKAVIM. YOU FASHIONED THE HUMAN BEING INTRICATE IN DESIGN.

Carrie knows that legions of aspiring parents have visited the mikveh center during her nine years of employment there. Many come to fulfill their duties as observant women. Jewish law mandates that women "purify" themselves after each menstrual cycle so they can resume sexual contact with their husbands. So they can make babies, in other words. Mikveh as a passport to procreation.

But Carrie's mikveh center embraces another kind of aspiring parent, one seeking solace in their struggle to conceive. The same pool of water in which the fertile submerge also purifies the barren and those who have miscarried and those who have undergone lifesaving late-term abortions. What does it feel like to need that kind of relief? To have to stare that kind of grief in the face?

She shows you a binder full of the center's ceremonies, several of which are tailored to the childless. They have been created collaboratively by a rabbi, a poet, and a psychologist, a trinity that tempts you to add *walk into a bar*, but there is nothing funny about their words, bound in waterproof sleeves:

- I acknowledge the losses and lessons of the past and I open my heart to the blessings yet to come.

- I will enter into this mikveh of living waters, this water-womb, as an act of closure and cleansing.

- I am ready to affirm life as it will now be.

Carrie felt the weight of their woe, was aware of it through all three of her pregnancies, and during three maternity leaves, and in between daily sessions pumping breast milk mere feet from visitors grieving in the pools. Maybe she felt a little guilt, too, in light of the ease with which she created a family. She didn't want more children, but her uterus was "collecting dust." Surely she could help. Couldn't she?

Nekavim nekavim. To ready Carrie's body to receive a fertilized egg, her husband, Jamie, gave her daily shots of Lupron, a synthetic hormone that suppresses ovulation. Then she moved on to twice-weekly estrogen shots to thicken her uterine lining, which Jamie administered into her backside via a needle she described on her blog as "the length of a yardstick." After which came the progesterone, one intramuscular shot each night for the first trimester.

Carrie gets anxious around needles, even at the thought of them. And she did the math: 129 injections, all told. To calm her nerves and mitigate the pain, she assembled ice packs and heating pads and engaged in the kind of regimented, Lamaze-style breathing you practiced during your own labors. She also repeated a mantra to remind herself that she'd endured worse: *I've given birth, I've given birth, I've given birth.*

Nekavim nekavim. You fashioned the human being so intricate in design that she can endure biotechnological feats and prepare for pregnancy by thinking about the agony of delivery.

* * *

This was not the beginning of Carrie's surrogacy process; it was the beginning only of the physical part. The endeavor began over a year before, when she filled out an application to an agency. Questions covered her income and education, but also her feelings about the "selective reduction" of multiples and termination (she supports either if it's the parents' preference). Some agencies inquire about an applicant's taste in music or favorite flower. Carrie's didn't. It did, however, ask if she'd ever been raped. Or had sex "even once" with a man who'd slept with another man, which I presume has to do with HIV susceptibility. It questioned her willingness to host more than one fetus (no) and her preferences about the parents for whom she was prepared to carry, including gay couples, unmarried couples, single folks (yes, yes, and yes). She drew the line at an HIV-positive parent. While medically safe, the prospect of being injected with genetic material from a carrier of the disease made her too uncomfortable.

Carrie also included something you suspect is unusual in a surrogacy application. A poem. And not just any poem, but one sourced from the floral-fabric-covered notebook she filled at summer camp. You saved your floral-fabric-covered notebook, too, if not for the words it contains then for the sense memories it evokes. You and your friends sprawled on bunk beds beside clip-on fans, hand-copying stanzas and song lyrics and quotations from one another's' pages, reading verses aloud, swooning over the sentiments expressed. The credits are a hodgepodge, a composite of verses written alternately by your teenage counselors and William Shakespeare. On one page, Bob Dylan and Shirley Temple. On the next, Tolstoy and Kermit the Frog.

For her application, Carrie selected a poem you don't have in your book, one you don't know, by a poet you've never heard of: "Jigsaw" by Lawrence Kushner. You wonder if your omission is significant. Prescient somehow. Why isn't it in your book too?

> Everyone carries with them at least one and probably
> Many pieces to someone else's puzzle.
> Sometimes they know it.
> Sometimes they don't.

Here's another question from Carrie's application: How can you reassure us that you would not change your mind about relinquishing the child?

I wouldn't be relinquishing it, Carrie typed. I'd be giving it to the people to whom it belongs.

There used to be only one kind of surrogate, a woman who donated both her egg and her uterus. This rendered her the genetic mother as well as the host. The practice has roots in the Old Testament. You know some biblical yarns, but you didn't remember that infertile Sarah, eager to procreate and getting on in years, suggested that Abraham sleep with her maid, Hagar. "It may be that I may obtain children by her," Sarah told her husband. (There's no mention of how Hagar felt about this.) The plan worked; Hagar begot Ishmael. But problems ensued. Hagar began to treat Sarah with "contempt," and Sarah, in turn, "dealt harshly" with Hagar.

This traditional arrangement remains problematic still, and came under serious scrutiny during the fight for custody of Baby M. In 1985, not long after in vitro fertilization enabled a woman to deliver an infant to whom she wasn't genetically related, the same year Margaret Atwood published *The Handmaid's Tale*, about women forced to serve as breeders, a New Jersey couple hired a surrogate named Mary Beth Whitehead. Mary Beth underwent artificial insemination with the intended father's sperm and, along with her own egg, conceived Baby M, whom she bore and surrendered to the couple. But Mary Beth was distraught. A few days later, she retrieved her biological daughter under the guise of a visit and absconded to Florida, where she was eventually found. The case made its way to the New Jersey Supreme Court. Protesters marched with signs. SURROGACY: IT'S INHUMAN!

Mary Beth insisted that surrogacy can't work. "Every mother who has ever lived understands the type of bond that takes place between her and her baby when she is carrying the child in her womb," she said in a court certification document. "It is real and it is powerful, and it is compelling."

Carrie doesn't feel a special connection to the baby kicking under her maternity shirt, partly because she knows, in no uncertain terms, that this is not her baby. But she didn't feel especially connected to her own kids in utero either. Neither did you, if you're being honest, despite finding the experience profound. Despite talking to and singing to your belly and rubbing the angular lumps of each son's limbs as he repositioned. Maybe it's because, like Carrie, you didn't lock in names beforehand or set up a nursery. Or maybe it's because your children were abstract until they were in the world. Invisible. For nine months, they were your body.

Custody of Baby M ultimately reverted to the intended parents, and Mary Beth received visitation rights. At age eighteen, no longer a baby, M severed legal ties with her biological mother.

Carrie's surrogacy agency wards against a Baby M–like scenario and other potential imbroglios through rigorous vetting: home visits, credit checks, psychological screenings. It green-lights just 2 percent of applicants—fewer than 50 surrogates are chosen out of the 2,400 or so who apply each year. It is the ultimate job interview. This, after all, is a job. The money piece troubles some folks, but Carrie thinks she deserves to be paid for what she calls her "extreme babysitting" gig, even if compensation's not her motivation. Her contract is confidential, but you gather that, excluding medical and legal expenses, she probably nets something like $30,000. (Or, for twenty-four hours a day, thirty days a month, over nine months: $4.62 per hour.)

Carrie's the executive director of the mikveh center. Her

husband helps direct a Jewish educational institution. They own a four-bedroom house on a charming cul-de-sac and have a live-in au pair. She doesn't need the income, she says; when she set out on this journey, she didn't even realize surrogates got paid. Still, it's a welcome bonus. She can finally start a college fund.

Such benevolence, you suspect, isn't what motivates all 2,400 applicants to Carrie's agency. In talking to friends, you have heard several stories of carriers making increasing off-the-record demands of intended parents who feared too much for their unborn children not to comply. Maybe, though, that's the other pole, the greed to Carrie's charity.

Nekavim nekavim. You fashioned the human being so intricate in design that it can fracture and fail in countless ways en route to childbirth. Surrogacy contracts enumerate them, and their corresponding values. Mandated bed rest might require the parents to pay an additional $250 per week. An invasive procedure like dilation and curettage, a scraping of the uterine lining, $1,500, the same amount awarded if you lose your fallopian tubes. A cesarean section could yield $2,500. A complete hysterectomy, perhaps $4,000. There's a range. But there's a ballpark too.

Reading the list gives you a queasy feeling not unlike the one you had when drafting your will. With whom would you leave your children if something befell you and your husband? And if those people perished, whom then? You consider how hard it was to move around after your own C-section, the painful infection that developed at the incision site, the numbness the area still retains. You consider a friend's suffering after a late-term abortion, and a fellow writer's placental abruption that left her hemorrhaging on a bathroom floor. The likelihood of a major complication is small, especially for Carrie (her track record! her success rate!). A car accident's more likely, and yet both of you drive.

Carrie seems undisturbed. Take out my uterus; I don't care, she says. I'm not having any more babies. You know?

You don't know. You don't know if you could be so casual about your uterus. It's not about future babies, not only. It's about the integrity of your body, which you are thoroughly scrubbing in the mikveh center shower.

Here's another clause in Carrie's contract: from twenty-four weeks on, she cannot visit her parents or grandparents on Long Island. The New Jersey Supreme Court invalidated commercial surrogacy contracts after the Baby M case, inspiring other states, like New York, to weigh in. If Carrie goes into labor on a familial visit, everyone from her to the agency to the clinic could be found guilty of a crime and saddled with fines of up to ten grand apiece.

Few places around the world permit commercial surrogacy, and laws vary, even within countries, sometimes within states. It is a criminal offense in most of Australia and Brazil, but legal in

India, where it's a massive industry that employs needy women. Canada, excluding Quebec, sanctions only altruistic surrogacy, in which the carrier is not compensated. Most of the European Union doesn't permit the practice at all. Nobody knows how many surrogacy arrangements exist, since the industry is unregulated. What is known is that many who want to hire surrogates must source them from elsewhere. Like Vivianne and David, who reside in the UK. Vivianne and David, who tried to conceive for over seven years and believe life without a child of their own is "missing meaning." Vivianne and David, who learn about Carrie, who lives in Massachusetts, where surrogacy agencies have figured out how to protect all parties involved.

Introductory emails are exchanged. A Skype session is scheduled. And after months of talk and contemplation, after theorizing and forecasting, after umpteen hours of research, Carrie meets real people, a flesh-and-blood husband and wife who want to create a family like hers.

It is awkward and thrilling. Everybody waves. Everyone is giddy.

Except, maybe, for Jamie. He is pleased, but wary. Not only will a strange man's baby be in his wife's body—a fact that is inherently uncomfortable—but there are medical what-ifs. There's the disruptive nature of pregnancy. At the same time, he is awed enough by his wife's wellspring of compassion not to interfere.

*   *   *

Carrie is officially matched to Vivianne and David. In August 2016, they fly to the US to meet her and also, as they say in the business, "to make their deposit." The fertility clinic winds up with several viable embryos. And on a Thursday, in January 2017, with Vivianne and David bearing witness over Skype, a catheter slips an embryo into Carrie's womb. A month later, all watch a black-and-white heart flickering on the ultrasound and listen to its muffled thump.

Nekavim nekavim.

And then, an error.

And then, a problem.

Carrie had developed a sensitivity to two antibodies while delivering her second child. She had made this clear to the agency. It was also included on the medical charts that the fertility clinic received. If the egg or the sperm of the would-be parents contains either of these antibodies, Carrie's immune system could perceive the fetus's blood as foreign and attack it. She had been assured this was a nonissue.

As a matter of routine, Carrie's obstetrician requests the fertility clinic's blood work, and a cursory glance reveals something disconcerting. David's sperm appears to be positive for one of the disallowed antibodies. A misprint? Carrie panics. New blood tests are ordered and the results are a worst-case scenario: both sperm and egg contain the antibody. Without question, the fetus in Carrie's womb has it too. The agency, it seems, didn't stress Carrie's sensitivity strongly enough. The fertility specialists didn't read her medical chart with care. Suddenly her pregnancy is very high risk.

Carrie is furious. And petrified. And confused. She sees a maternal-fetal medicine specialist, who explains they'll need to monitor her blood. If the antibody levels rise, which is probable, and an ultrasound confirms increased blood flow to the baby's brain—a sign of hemolytic disease, like severe anemia—the baby will require an intrauterine blood transfusion while Carrie's under epidural anesthesia. Actually, the baby will require an intrauterine blood transfusion every fourteen or so days, since that's as long as each one's effective. Presuming she can make it to thirty-four weeks without an emergency C-section—she is ten weeks along at this point—she will deliver a premature baby, who will likely need additional blood transfusions and will be promptly admitted to the neonatal intensive care unit.

Vivianne and David are there for this revelation, too, on Skype. The doctor can't determine the probability of this scenario, he says, but it wouldn't surprise him if it came to pass. After all, the fetus has the antibodies, positively.

Carrie has never had an epidural; she gets woozy at the thought of a giant needle in her spine. Also, she has a full-time job. And three young children. And her hospital's an hour from home. Suddenly her situation seems absurdly treacherous and unwieldy. This was not supposed to happen. She tries not to show the parents how shaken she is. How frightened.

Then, from the screen, Vivianne lets out a yelp. It is not, Carrie realizes with alarm, a sound of concern. It is a cheer. A woot. Vivianne has endured multiple miscarriages and losses and false starts, has tried technologies in multiple countries, and to her the data passing over the doctor's lips and across the ocean and into her ears reassembles into only one thing. Life. When all is said and done, the infant will survive.

We're having a baby! Vivianne screams, fists pumping.

4. *B'TZELEM ELOHIM.*
I AM MADE IN THE IMAGE OF ~~GOD~~.

You do not say this to yourself in the bathroom where, post-shower, you have wrapped yourself in an oversize white sheet. Carrie has given you a Sharpie with which to modify your printed mikveh ceremony, and you use it to delete every appearance of the word *God*. It is lead on your tongue—immovable, indigestible.

This is not what you were taught at camp. There, you learned how after God created man in his image, He gave his first commandment: "Be fruitful and multiply." It is the law many ultra-Orthodox rabbis cite when prohibiting birth control or sanctioning divorce for couples who cannot reproduce. It is also one that Jamie respects. Carrie was content with two children. Jamie suggested they try for a third. He wanted to do more than just replace themselves after they were gone. There are Jewish genocides to account for, a long history of butchery and forced conversions. Procreation assures preservation.

Carrie doesn't disagree. In fact, she thinks reproductive technology offers new ways to satisfy the command. She knows that some observant Jews think that if a couple is infertile, it must be God's will, and who is man—or woman—to interfere? But Carrie believes in God's will too. She believes it's God's will that someone like her will come along and offer to carry their baby.

B'tzelem Elohim. You are made in the image of your mother and father.

Still dripping, you wander into the adjacent room—a small, dim, private space with a comfortable chair and a telephone. You are following instructions printed on a page you carry with you. Here's your next one: "Lift the receiver and dial 200." The number will ring Alyse in the reception area. You will tell her you are ready for the pool.

Some visitors want supervision to ensure that their immersion is valid, that their entire bodies, including the upper reaches of their hair, submerge. Mikveh guides respect modesty by hiding behind a sheet—hence, your toga—lowering it only to assess a plunge, then raising it again. But you have opted to immerse unsupervised. This is what you will tell Alyse. You will not tell her that the legitimacy of the immersion doesn't concern you, that you're doing this just to sate your curiosity about Carrie, about yourself. Nor will you tell her that your period is a few days late, that it's been a bit irregular lately, that when it didn't come on time last month you panicked your way through an internet search for a place to terminate, even as the thought of snuffing out an embryo—that could grow into someone you'd love as much as you do your sons—left you sleepless. Still, you cannot cope with the prospect of another pregnancy, another child, another infant with the temperament of your second-born: six straight months of untreatable colic, of wailing with such volume and persistence that your upstairs neighbors threatened to call the cops. (What did they think was going on?) You and your husband took turns going mad and reassuring your two-year-old that his baby brother wasn't in pain. (Wasn't he?)

You punch 2-0-0 on the keypad, and as the line rings, you feel the urge to make a joke. *I am naked and ready for you*, you could say with a sultry twinge. Or maybe something in a deep and lordly baritone, since this is a holy call. The whole situation feels a bit absurd to your cynical self.

The call goes to voice mail. Nobody's available, says the recording. You try again, jokes retreating. Again, no luck. You glance around the room, scan brochures on a side table encouraging women to stand up to abuse, to seek help. "You are not alone." You leave a message. Hi, Alyse. It's Courtney. You have not been told what to do in this case, have not been told how to proceed in this place of multistep processes. You are standing in a dark suite, dripping wet and wrapped in a largely unabsorbent sheet.

* * *

B'tzelem Elohim. Vivianne and David, practicing Jews, want to ensure that their child is made in the image of their God. According to the rabbis they consult, a Jewish egg plus Jewish sperm will not necessarily a Jewish baby make if the oven in which the embryo is cooked is not Jewish too. This pronouncement prolonged Vivianne and David's path to conception. Apparently there is a scarcity of Jewish surrogates.

Carrie consulted a rabbi, too, when her interest in gestational surrogacy took hold. Was this undertaking kosher? What did Jewish law have to say on the subject? That's how she learned that it's frowned upon for a Jewish woman to deliver a child who won't be raised Jewish, even if she's unrelated to the baby. Carrie respects Jewish law far more than you do. And so her course was set. She would serve as a surrogate for a Jewish couple.

Carrie once imagined helping a couple a lot like her and Jamie—laid-back, forward-thinking, allegiant Jews—and becoming buddies with them, a fantasy reinforced by her Facebook surrogacy group, where carriers routinely describe their intended parents as their "perfect match." But when the Skype call in the high-risk doctor's office ends, Carrie is in tears. She is terrified of what may come to pass with her pregnancy, but also, she feels indescribably disconnected from this jubilant couple whose child is in her body.

Back home, with reassurance from Jamie that she can do this, that she has his full support, Carrie looks into the financial significance of the news. She may need upward of six epidurals for six transfusions, and, according to the contract, each surgical procedure equates to something like $1,500, though Carrie can't tell you the actual amount because her contract mandates confidentiality. She alerts the agency and the parents so they can be prepared, just in case. There is pushback. The transfusion's not surgery, says the agency. In fact, the word *transfusion* is not in the contract at all, and while the situation is regrettable, there's no line item to account for it. Vivianne and David email her to say they're saving up to fly to Boston for the birth and they can't pay her additional monies, and they're really sorry and fingers crossed and please understand.

Carrie is appalled. She feels misused. She feels, she says, like a "robot uterus." She's really expected to brave this ordeal at her own expense?

You are stunned too. You think acts of extreme generosity should be rewarded with extreme gratitude, even extreme sums. Why don't Vivianne and David have reserves for this sort of thing? Don't they know the unpredictability of pregnancy? Isn't that an essential part of the contract they signed? You think, too, about the gross unfairness of a compassionate act met with so little compassion.

You wonder if the clinic's negligence and her physical peril and Vivianne and David's behavior have tarnished Carrie's experience. Jiggered her point of view. Because all of it has cemented yours. If there was ever a microscopic sliver of an open window onto this possibility for you, it has been closed and locked.

* * *

A few months have passed since she despaired in the specialist's office, and the antibody levels in her blood haven't spiked. She hasn't needed aggressive treatments. This has softened Carrie. But she's also thoughtful and forgiving. *B'tzelem Elohim.* She doesn't know how it would affect her to try and fail to conceive for seven years. It might scar her. Change her. Blind her to someone else's fear and pain. Not to mention that Vivianne's never been pregnant, she says. Maybe she doesn't appreciate what it means to have an epidural. It is folly to hold a grudge. So she doesn't.

She does consult a lawyer about the clinic's negligence, but learns that to file a lawsuit, there need to be assessable damages, and so far she's medically in the clear. And while she thinks about going after them for pain and suffering, she determines that it will only induce more of the same.

5. *ELOHAI NESHAMA SHENATATA BI TEHORAH HI.* THE SOUL IN ME IS PURE.

Nora slept on a bunk below yours at camp when you were eleven or twelve. One morning, early in the summer, you woke to find her face inches from yours. As a kid, Nora had had a stroke that left one side of her body bigger than the other. Her shoes were different sizes, her legs different lengths. She walked with a limp. Nora often gawked at things with her mouth ajar. This is how she appeared to you that weekday morning when your eyes opened to her magnified face.

You look beautiful when you sleep, she said, drool pooled in her bottom lip.

Stop staring at me! you shouted. In the same moment, you realized that she was naked, en route to the shower. Also, that she was a woman: full breasts and pubic hair to your mosquito bites and fuzz. You don't remember adding *Go away!*, but you probably did. You do remember telling all your friends what Nora said and how she looked, and how, for the rest of the summer, you limped behind her back, head tilted, tongue lolling. *You look beautiful when you sleep.* You were ruthless. Carrie was too. Nora asked you both to stop. Please. She was always polite about it. The memory stalks you both. You spill your shame in Carrie's kitchen. You were old enough to know better. You knew better. But you did it anyway.

Sometimes, Nora appears in your dreams. Just her pale, soft face, wet lips parted. She doesn't speak. Neither do you. Instead, you study each other. You hope you are dreaming up a kinder version of yourself, hope your eyes hold in them some kind of apology she can discern. Though you are connected on social media, you have never had the guts to say you're sorry.

At the café where you sit with Carrie, she takes a picture with you, captions it "Twelve years since we've seen each other?," posts it on Facebook.

Nora "likes" it with a heart.

Elohai neshama shenatata bi tehorah hi. The soul in me is pure? You think there's probably only one subset of the population whose souls are pure, assuming there's such a thing as souls, assuming there's such a thing as purity: newborns.

6. ~~KOL HANESHAMA T'HALEL YAH.~~ ~~THE BREATH OF EVERY LIVING~~ ~~THING PRAISES YOU~~.

Every living thing except for you, apparently, since you cross out this one too.

Leading up to your visit to the mikveh, you deliberated over an occasion worthy of immersion, scrolled through suggestions on the mikveh center's website, including: losing a loved one, celebrating a birthday, coming out of the closet. You weighed the matters that keep you up at night: your son's anxiety, your other son's asthma, your father's cancer, a fascist president, environmental cataclysm, racism, anti-Semitism, terrorism, war. But here, with Carrie, you are preoccupied with motherhood. With your own and hers and Vivianne's and that of all women who have immersed or will immerse in the same small pool.

And then it occurs to you. When you and your husband decided not to have any more children, you thought only about what it wouldn't mean for your life. A daughter whose hair you could braid, a gaggle of children who outnumbered their parents, a crowded apartment, savings diluted. By considering only what wouldn't be, you thought little about what would be. About what is. You did not, for example, dwell on what it meant for your body.

Case in point: you breastfed each of your sons for over a year, an activity you loved physically and nutritionally but loathed logistically. You couldn't go more than a few hours without nursing or strapping on an electric pump. The demand was immense. All those random places where you wound up shirtless, the pump's emphatic engine groaning: a restaurant bathroom, a parked car, your office while students queued up outside the door. Once you had to breastfeed your crying son on a subway platform bench, and a urine-soaked homeless man pointed at your half-exposed breasts and fondled his crotch.

Shortly after your youngest moved to a bottle, you smoked a single cigarette on the fire escape to assert that no one else's health depended on your intake.

And then your children were toddlers and preschoolers, and nursing was simply something you used to do.

You will immerse to acknowledge a transition you never properly articulated. That your womb will no longer house children. That your breasts will no longer feed them. That your shoulders and back and hips will no longer support an infant in a sling. That your children will no longer depend on you—and you will no longer serve them—in the same primal ways.

The realization makes your eyes well up, even though you've known it all along. Even though it has already happened.

Carrie suggests a ceremony on weaning, and though your occasion is more encompassing, the language requires little modification.

As I prepare myself for this immersion, I look in the mirror and notice the ways that my body has been transformed by the act of creating and nourishing new life.

You look. You see.

You say, I am grateful ~~to God~~ for my body's amazing capacity to grow and sustain life. Now I prepare to reclaim my body for myself, to sustain my good health and my well-being and to nourish my own spirit.

On your third unsuccessful phone call to reception, you crack open the door of your preparation suite and step into the sunlit anteroom. Hello? Your voice ricochets off the walls and lofted ceiling. Through a doorway you see Alyse chatting with someone and you retreat back into the suite, where the phone rings.

Sorry, Alyse says. I was with a guest. You imagine said guest was confessing the purpose of her visit, and Alyse couldn't step away. *I just miscarried. I just survived uterine cancer. I am barren. I am childless. I am broken. Is there a ceremony for that?*

Carrie had explained that the ceremonies offer enhancements to the immersion ritual, a way to infuse the experience with additional meaning. The word *mikveh* denotes simply a "gathering" of water and appears in the Good Book when God gathers waters to create the world. This makes most natural (a.k.a. divine) bodies of water mikvehs. Oceans are mikvehs— the world's biggest. You love this fact. The ocean is a mikveh!

Because access to natural water can pose a challenge for regular visitors and interfere with a woman's commitment to modesty, Jewish life necessitates man-made pools, the construction of which must adhere to precise specifications. A mikveh must be built into the ground, for one, and fashioned from certain materials and be large enough to hold something like 150 gallons of water, most of which can come from the tap, but a portion of which must be naturally occurring. As such, the external perimeter of this mikveh center is a channel that accumulates precipitation. It shares a common wall with the pools, and a pipe enables outside water to intermingle with inside water or, in the words of Jewish law, allows the waters to "kiss."

Instruction: "Enter the room with the mikveh pool through a door inside the suite. Drop your sheet."

"Say, 'As I enter the living waters of the mikveh, I am mindful of each step on the journey of birthing and raising a child.'"

The pool's the size of a large Jacuzzi, the water about ninety-eight degrees, a heated blanket on your feet. After the seven-step descent, it envelops you up to your chest. You lift your feet and bob.

Instruction: "Reach for the red handle on the wall to let in a burst of rain, then twist it closed."

Here's another mikveh rule. You must immerse three times. It is generally understood that one plunge might be an accident, two a coincidence. Three times designates intention. One rabbi who supervises conversions recommends, on the mikveh center's website, that on the first immersion you regard the past; the second, the present; and the third, the future.

You don't do this, not exactly, but with each dunk, you do think about your sons and your womb and the ways in which your midsection grew and shrank like a durable balloon, and how you grew flesh-and-blood human beings inside you and made the singular substance on which they lived and thrived, and how wild it is that your body was able to do that, that your body did that, that your body will never do that again. You cannot help but think about Carrie's body, doing that again.

"When you resurface, say, 'I call to mind the holiness of the body.'"

Carrie doesn't think the mikveh creates tangible change, even if some entries in the guestbook suggest otherwise. ("I emerged the person I always wanted to be," wrote one visitor.) It won't make the infertile fertile, or provide lasting peace to the suffering. Instead, it is a forced pause, a way to delineate where you are on your journey. It is a bookmark you slip in between pages to ruminate over what you read, to interpret the story's significance, its power.

As for water, the Old Testament teems with symbolic stories: the Red Sea parting as Jews pass from enslavement to freedom, a flood that cleanses the world of evil. Water is a transitional element, Carrie says. You think, too, about the pool inside the womb, about a fetus sucking oxygen from its mother's—or carrier's—every breath. About the passage from bound to unbound with the cutting of the cord.

You towel off and dress and return to Carrie's office, where the two of you eat fruit salad and laugh at a camp photo in which she is wearing your dress and you are wearing hers. How guileless those young faces seem. How little you knew about the lives you'd lead.

7. *TIKKUN OLAM.*
WE CAN STAND FOR JUSTICE;
WE CAN BUILD A WORLD
OF PEACE AND JUSTICE.

Carrie wants to convince more women to step up as gestational surrogates. It is a cruel fate, she thinks, that some couples are fertile and others are not, and surrogacy offers a kind of rectification. To inspire potential candidates, or at least generate conversation in the Jewish community on an underdiscussed subject, she starts a blog where she reveals the ups and downs of her experience, though not in as much detail as she might like, since Vivianne and David might read it. You don't ask if she thinks readers will be put off by the challenges she braved. Maybe they won't. Maybe that's just you.

Isn't it tempting to be someone's hero? An antidote to existential unhappiness? *Tikkun olam?* But for the costs. But for the body. But for childbirth, which drew out of you animalistic shrieks so loud the nurses said they could hear you from their station down the hall.

What about the look in Vivianne's and David's eyes when you give them the newborn? Carrie might say. *And the knowledge that you brought forth what they wanted most in the world? Think about how much you love your children,* she might add. *Think about how profound it would be, how amazing it would feel, to sow the seeds of that love for someone else.*

Here's how you imagine it might feel: You would be hypersensitive to people talking about your glow and your shape, to their congratulations. You would be too eager to have such praise apply to you, and disturbed that it doesn't. (*But wouldn't it?* Carrie might say. *Aren't you glowing?*) You would be unnerved by ultrasound images of a fetus that resembles your sons in utero, since sonogram pictures look so similar. You would be distraught in the hospital when, after a year and a half of psychological and emotional and physical strain, after a fierce and exhausting delivery, after full breasts that would never get expressed, after bleeding through maxi pads the size of diapers, after ambling down the hall past a glass-walled nursery full of impossibly tiny, silken faces, you would head home with nothing but your purse.

Carrie, meanwhile, can't imagine taking home a newborn. Her family is full. She doesn't have the bandwidth, she says, to deal with the strains of infancy and toddlerhood, of preschooler tantrums and negotiations, especially since she has other children who need her attention. Pregnancy is temporary. Parenthood is not.

It isn't that the process would make you yearn for another child. It's that you don't have faith in your ability to weather the hormonal fluctuations that follow birth, or the pain of your body healing without a newborn to nuzzle. During the postpartum period, you were alternately euphoric and anxious and vanquished, sometimes all at once. But you are not Carrie. You are not as pragmatic or even-keeled. You cannot compartmentalize as well as she does; the boundaries between your compartments leak. And, unlike for her, the rewards, the gratification of goodwill, would not outweigh the costs.

Are there compassionate acts you perform that would seem unimaginable to her? Surely nothing of this caliber.

Tikkun olam? Remember Sarah, Abraham's barren wife? The Lord eventually shows her mercy. At ninety, thirteen or so years after relying on a surrogate, she finally conceives baby Isaac. It is the kind of supernatural justice that doesn't befall infertile couples in the known world, even if they're patient and prayerful, even if they visit the mikveh. The kind of justice that seems possible only with technology—and someone like Carrie.

The prospect of Sarah's late-stage motherhood makes her laugh; when it later comes true, she declares, "All that hear will laugh with me." Likely not laughing, though, is Hagar. Sarah is disapproving of Abraham's surrogate family, and doesn't want

Ishmael "[to] be heir with my son, even with Isaac." She implores Abraham to "cast out this bondwoman and her son" into the wilderness. And he reluctantly obliges. Pretty soon Hagar and Ishmael are lost in the woods and out of food and water. Hagar breaks down. She cannot bear to see her son suffer, does not want to watch him die. Alas, an angel swoops in and saves them both.

It is hard not to think about the role surrogacy plays in the Old Testament—a text that shapes Carrie's daily life. This book is the reason she eats only kosher food and why, on Saturdays, she doesn't drive or cook or use the phone. It is the foundation for the mikveh center—her livelihood—and the justification for having three children instead of two, and why the couple for whom she's serving as a surrogate had to be Jewish.

You hoped that these pages in which she finds wisdom and guidance would have something meaningful to say on surrogacy, since they feature several women struggling with infertility. What they offer instead is Sarah's laughter alongside her banished surrogate's sobs. You cannot reconcile these narratives. Hagar likely had no choice but to "lay" with her boss. Is that not an extreme act worthy of appreciation? Surely the burdens of pregnancy and delivery haven't changed with time. If anything, modern science has made women more comfortable.

Perhaps the biblical story is a lesson in how *not* to treat women who help the infertile. A lesson in respecting surrogate mothers.

Of course, Carrie's story is not Hagar's. She sought out surrogacy long before she knew of Vivianne and David, and she pursued this route on her own. Moreover, she's not the baby's mother. Nor did she have sex with the father.

The spare text of the Old Testament leaves ample room for interpretation and extrapolation, and you are not a rabbi or a scholar; your vantage point is limited and incomplete. But what's clear to you, what seems inarguable, is a timeless desire for biological children. As a reader of Genesis, you first pity barren Sarah, then seethe on behalf of Hagar. You sympathize with Vivianne and David's fundamental despair, and also resent how oblivious of Carrie they seem.

Another friend of yours struggled to conceive but forewent technological intervention because of the bioethical issues it raised. Instead, she and her husband, both Jewish, adopted two children from developing countries, children whom they've loved and raised as their own. Children who are their own. She doesn't understand surrogacy. She doesn't understand why, with the treasury of unwanted children on our overpopulated planet, infertile couples wouldn't pursue adoption instead. Why are folks so concerned with procreation?

You empathize with her—it's impossible not to; you know her kids—and can only attribute it to an innate urge that strikes many, that struck you: an urge to create a family from the love you share with your partner. You are lucky you could. You take such ease for granted.

What would you have done if you couldn't get pregnant?

How far would you have gone? In vitro? Donor sperm? Donor egg? Would you have hired a surrogate? How much is a biological child worth to you—financially? emotionally?—and at what point would you have regarded adoption? Would you have realized you could simultaneously become a parent and change a parentless child's life? The only way for you to answer these questions would be to have had another life. The necessity of your biological motherhood could have been determined only by biological incapacity.

Tikkun. Justice. Or, more accurately, a "fixing." A word with manifold meanings in every language. For parents. For women. For Jews. You will spend the next several months—and likely the rest of your life—considering your relationship to restoration, and also how you can cultivate compassion in your sons. You will think about this when you take them to rallies denouncing xenophobia and racism and when you answer their questions about anti-Semitism and misogyny. You will think about this when you teach literature about love and suffering, and when the act of reading stokes students' empathy, and when you write to unravel knots in your own understanding. You will always think about how there's more that you can do.

On her blog, Carrie quotes Rabbi Rachel Kobrin's "A Modern Prayer for a Surrogate Mother," words she read moments before a fertilized egg was transferred into her uterus. Here's the opening:

Makor HaChayim, Source of Life,
Inspire me to become a holy vessel, blessed with the
opportunity to carry this precious seed, providing
nourishment and warmth within the deep embrace of
my womb.

You are especially moved by verse three:

Rekindle within me the courage, for in holding this seed,
I am not merely making a child—I am also creating a
mother and a father. I am forming a family. And within
that family, a whole universe of possibility dwells.

You have heeded the meditations. You have followed
instructions.

Now: dwell in possibility.

IT MAY ALL
END IN ALEPPO

IN MY ALEPPO, THE coffee was bitter, the figs supple, and the evergreens open-crowned. I gorged on pita and labneh and after every meal, I smoked a pipe of shisha and watched mint-scented clouds swell and scatter.

I rode an eastbound tram from al-Jamiliyah to Bab al-Faraj, tracing the skyline out the window with my finger: up and down spires, up and over domes. Everything was the color of oatmeal, and the sky was an electric blue. I zigzagged through a fourteenth-century souk with vaulted, honeycombed ceilings and lost myself among mounds of spices. I passed cooked sheep heads, teeth intact in their semi-smiles, and pyramids of pottery, and rug stacks taller than their merchants. I passed a stall devoted entirely to brooms. It was hard not to think of the Silk Road on which the Syrian city had been a central stop. Especially when someone trotted by on a donkey.

Of course, this was the Aleppo of the 1960s, well before I was born. And as a young American woman, I likely couldn't have done these things. But I did. I went to all these places. I picked pomegranates from local shrubs and tucked them into my pockets.

2016: The faces of Aleppo flicker on our eyelids en route to sleep. That wide-eyed boy, skin and hair talcum-powdered with debris. A sea of anemone fingers grasping at rations. Sopping corpses, 230 all told, lined up like tombs after locals pulled them from the Queiq River.

One image forces my eyelids open: a red-shirted toddler, chubby cheek pressed into the sand, lips a figure eight, water lapping at his forehead. He is the same size as my two-year-old. He has washed ashore on the Greek island of Kos after fleeing from a city just north of Aleppo, as has his five-year-old brother. I have a five-year-old too.

Aleppo, a.k.a. Halab. So named, legend says, after Abraham tramped through with a flock of sheep and distributed their milk—*halav*—to the city's poor.

Aleppo: recorded in the Good Book as part of the extended area of Israel.

Aleppo: eponym of the world's oldest, most accurate and complete copy of the Hebrew Bible, the Aleppo Codex. Jews there preserved it in a safe, inside a rock, beneath the Great Synagogue, for six hundred years.

I met Sol in 2006, in a windowless Midtown Manhattan office, one whose small conference room was crammed with clothing racks. Sol owned an apparel business, which is how we connected. My friend, a journalist, had interviewed him for an article on retail trends. Afterward, Sol inquired about writers who might be interested in penning his memoir.

Enter the freshly minted MFA in need of a job.

Sol had side-combed silver hair and ruddy cheeks; absent his Arabic accent, he might've been mistaken for a Westerner. He seemed disappointed that I didn't know anything about Aleppo. Aren't you Jewish? he asked. (The Syrian city had been a polestar for the Sephardim.) I am, I said. I didn't tell him I'd resented having to attend Hebrew school in adolescence. That my bat mitzvah had proved memorable mostly because a friend made out with the boy I liked. How I was still waiting to believe in God. Instead, I offered assurances. I'm a diligent researcher, I said, a quick study.

A lanky, yarmulke-wearing employee barged into the conference room without knocking and muttered something to Sol in Arabic. The man's eyes scanned me, then darted away. His face suppressed a smile. I'd received a similar reaction in the reception area, a spate of awkward glances and smirks. Clarity would come later. How the Syrian Jews in Henry's domain, those reared in a majority-Muslim country, seemed to accept the Arabic designation for women: *haram*. Forbidden. How Sol and his staff—all male—observed a sect of Judaism that limited interaction with the opposite sex. At the very least, I should not have worn a tank top, despite the oppressive summer heat. My bare shoulders made them squirm.

Aleppo, the city Othello names just before stabbing himself in the gut.

Aleppo, whose mention in *Othello* inspired Nabokov's story "That in Aleppo Once..."

The link? Heroes in both narratives struggle to distinguish between what's real and what's imagined.

I interviewed Sol for hours at a time over many weeks, in his Midtown office, over the phone, in his brick house on Brooklyn's Ocean Parkway. The more he spoke, the less I understood. His childhood neighbors belonged to esoteric Muslim and Christian and sects whose names I could barely pronounce, let alone describe. The regimes under whose laws his family suffered fell every few months, in one coup after another. Even Aleppo's architecture spoke to a mesh of influences I couldn't parse. I wandered library aisles agog: theology, geography, political science. My book piles ballooned. Two months of writing became four, became six.

Sometimes I'd submit a section and Sol would wag his finger, shake his head. I don't think you're working very hard, he'd say. I don't think you've been listening.

I could've blamed an inadequate tongue. I speak only English and a smidgen of Spanish. Sol traded off among English and Arabic and Hebrew. He dreamed in French. I could have confessed that I skipped world history in high school in favor of ceramics. But then I'd hand over a section and he would slap his forehead in delight. You've penetrated my brain, he'd say. It's like you're seeing through my eyes.

How to know what would resonate? His memories commingled with my research and presumptions and inventions. His narrative, my sieve. His words in my mouth.

What was real? What was imagined? Everything. Nothing.

In 2014, warring blocs in the Battle of Aleppo merged and parted and re-formed. While TV reporters struggled to keep track—the al-Tawhid Brigade, the Salafi jihadists, the al-Nusra Front—I peered over their on-screen shoulders. There, the pillar atop which Saint Simeon preached for nearly forty years. There, the Baron Hotel, where Agatha Christie penned *Murder on the Orient Express*.

I nursed my newborn son and watched palm fronds on the skyline wobble in the wind, the static photos in my books suddenly inspired. Aleppo! I thought. Aleppo was alive.

* * *

This much may seem unlikely, but it's true: Aleppan Jews had a rich spiritual life in the mid-1900s. Sol had attended a yeshiva—albeit an underground one—and studied with the foremost scholars, vestiges of the city's Semitic roots. His family kept kosher, observed the Sabbath, went to shul.

I wish I could say religion bonded us, eclipsed our differences, but Sol and I knew different Judaisms—he, Orthodox Sephardic; I, Reform Ashkenazi. We spoke a few of the same Hebrew phrases, but in our respective accents the words didn't match. Our common holidays were feted with different customs. And while we knew some of the same timeworn songs, we sang them to different tunes.

What we did share were stories. Moses freeing the Jews from bondage in Egypt. Esther, queen of Persia, foiling Haman's plan to annihilate our ancestors. A flood that cleansed the earth of violence, sparing only Noah and his ark. What we shared was faith in tenacity. In resolve. In the olive branch Noah's dove retrieved from an earth reborn.

In my Aleppo, the Citadel, ostensibly the world's oldest castle, presided over the Old City from atop a giant hill. Its limestone steps had summoned Greeks and Romans. Each archway framed a different view. Ramparts. Courtyards. Domes aligned like breasts. I paused at a shrine for the Mesopotamian god Hadad, protector of life, and again at the fortified gates.

I traipsed through secret passageways designed to dupe the enemy. So many ways to stay safe.

But I'm telling you only the dream.

At the base of the Citadel hung a sign: NO PESTS ALLOWED. The accompanying illustration was a caricature of a hook-nosed Jew.

There were ten thousand Jews in Aleppo in 1947, when Sol was born. The exodus began months after his birth, with the UN's decision to partition Palestine. Mobs torched Jewish homes and schools and the Great Synagogue, slayed seventy-five supposed Zionists. *Al-haraek*, Aleppans would call it. The fires.

Sol and his family might have been consumed, too, had it not been for a Muslim neighbor. Try another block, the man told the approaching crowd. There aren't Jews here. He knew, of course, that on the other side of the wall behind him, Sol's parents were willing their infant son not to cry.

Jews fled in droves after *al-haraek*, and not just because they dreaded more conflagration. Their fear was greater. Mystical. Rumors had spread that when the Great Synagogue smoldered, so did the Aleppo Codex, a parchment that was said to have magical powers. Young women who gazed upon it became pregnant, locals said. Men in trouble who prayed before it could have their luck restored. And those who held keys to the safe that housed it were divinely blessed.

Likewise, if the Codex suffered harm, a plague would befall the community in charge of protecting it. By 1959, just two thousand Jews remained in Aleppo. By 1967, there were half as many.

Still, Sol's recalcitrant parents refused to budge. They were old, tired. They'd worked hard to establish a life in their city and didn't know where else to go. Sanctions intensified. Jews could no longer own cars or homes or phones. They endured a 10 p.m. curfew and identifying stamps on their IDs. By 1971, Halabi Jews were confined to a 3.5-mile-wide patch of city and threatened with death if they tried to flee.

But that summer, twenty-four-year-old Sol did.

I had fantasized about visiting Aleppo, a city into which I imagined my way. When its structures crumbled, when its people cried out, I felt ravaged as I suspect others in my circles did not. The destruction felt personal.

But what did I really know of Aleppo? What could I say about honeysuckle flowers I had never smelled? About a sun whose warmth I had never felt on my face? The only Aleppan I ever got to know was Sol.

Sol didn't know about the Holocaust, not until he was a grown man. Not until he left. He'd heard rumors, murmurs in his boyhood, but it seemed impossible. How could six million people perish? By what means? In Syria, muzzled reporters skated over it. Books by local authors excluded it. Sol's history texts favored descriptions of Arab nationalism over anti-Semitism. What to make, then, of Syria harboring Nazi war criminal Alois Brunner, architect of the Final Solution? It's just as well that his family didn't know how Brunner repaid his hosts: by sharing the torture tactics he used under Hitler.

Some of Sol's declarations seemed implausible, but I couldn't know for sure. I was the first person in Aleppo in forty years to run away, he told me. I graduated from college as the best student in all of Syria, he said. These statements might have raised red flags or led me to dismiss other recollections as hyperbolic, if not fantastic. But they didn't. Maybe it's because he had an elephantine memory for details about his home city, all of which were verifiable. Or maybe it was because he could summon his 1971 flight with painstaking precision.

Take away the minaret of Aleppo's Great Mosque, poised for 1,200 years like a finger pointing at the sky. Take away the National Museum and the curators who sheltered inside it, shuttling cuneiform tablets into its basement, trying to preserve civilization amid savagery. Take away the rug stalls and sheep heads and whole slabs of the Citadel: its grand steps, its fortress walls.

Take away every hospital in the city. Take away thirty-one thousand Aleppan lives.

Remove a million of the city's remaining inhabitants—half the population—and ten million more from the rest of the country. Sprinkle them like ashes across the globe. Watch them settle in the nooks: Greece, Germany, Canada. Arizona, Illinois, New York.

Hear their wide vowels. Let their soft *sh*s quiver in your ears.

I was sponging a tomato sauce stain off my son's high chair when I heard the news on CNN: the last Jews in Aleppo had been saved. It was October 2015. I squinted at the screen half expecting to see the names of Sol's parents, to see images of the faces I'd assembled one detail at a time. Instead I saw an elderly mother and her two daughters, one of whom would be denied passage into Israel because she'd married a Muslim and converted. Mariam Halabi, eighty-eight, would have to leave that daughter behind.

The reporter said there was no electricity in the part of Aleppo where Mariam and her Jewish daughter, Sarah, lived. Water was scarce. The women sensed that Assad's army was inching closer. In fact, when rebel forces pounded on their door in the middle of the night to transport them to safety, Mariam and Sarah presumed they were about to be arrested—or worse. Their fear was warranted. In the last moments of Aleppo's battle the following year, when all remaining residents were presumed enemies of Assad, Syrian troops simply charged into civilians' homes and slaughtered them.

Mariam's rescue mission had been arranged without her knowledge or permission. Her son Yoni in New York had called his local rabbi with concerns about his family in Aleppo, and the rabbi had contacted anti-Assad activist Moti Kahana, who in turn rang his contacts in Syria, who hatched a plan.

Two photos from the undertaking filled the screen. In one Mariam was in bed, silver hair disheveled, mouth agape, as though she'd been awoken, as if this were the very moment when she was told it was time to go. In another, she was walking arm-in-arm with men whose faces were blurred out. She looked frail in an oversize blue blazer, a patterned scarf wrapped around her head so that she might pass for a Muslim. She looked forlorn. She was missing teeth.

The driver of the getaway car took a circuitous route to the Turkish border to avoid military checkpoints. After a stop in Istanbul, the women made their way to a coastal city north of Tel Aviv.

Clearly Mariam needed aid. And surely it was preferable to save one daughter than to gamble on the lives of both. Wasn't it? Like some sort of alternate *Sophie's Choice*?

Aleppo, Halab, Aram Tzovah in the Old Testament. I envisioned the Jewish cemeteries nobody would visit. The pews in which nobody would pray.

Sponge. High chair. I scrubbed until my shoulder ached. The stains refused to dull.

Miraculously, the Codex didn't burn. (An act of God?) After *al-haraek*, community leaders picked through the ashes of the Great Synagogue, assembled the Codex's scattered pages, and re-hid them. Over a decade later, it was secreted away to Israel. Aleppo's crown, as it's known, now resides in the Shrine of the Book at the Israel Museum, in Jerusalem.

I can't tell you too much about Sol's escape—the story is his, not mine—but I can tell you this. It was Hollywoodish. It involved a Bedouin disguise and a cigarette smuggler. It entailed hiking over mountains and riding in a tractor trailer beneath rows of shitting sheep. It required aid from a synagogue community in Beirut and secret signals in a strange Lebanese café and an Israeli Navy torpedo boat. Eventually he made safe passage to Haifa and emigrated to the States.

We hadn't spoken in a decade, but I found myself back with him, in his office, in his living room, in his Aleppo, when consuming never-ending news of the war. I dug up his number, dialed. He seemed pleased to hear from me—and stunned to hear about my life.

I never thought you'd have a family, he said. You seemed like such a rebel.

Me? I said. Really?

He couldn't explain why he'd thought this. Perhaps he'd

thought it rebellious to be a secular Jew? To wear a tank top? I was in disbelief. How little did he know me? How little did we know each other?

He said it broke his heart to see what had happened to his birthplace, that he still thought of Aleppo as the most beautiful city in the world.

It is, I wanted to say. *It was.* Instead I asked what he thought about the political climate in his adopted home, about our shared president's stance on immigration.

You're a writer and an Ashkenazi, he said. Of course you hate Trump.

You shouldn't generalize, I replied. I was, after all, a rebel.

When you study Talmud, Sol said, you learn the art of deduction.

I could tell where this was going and my stomach clenched. You voted for him, didn't you? I said.

He doesn't mean everything he says, Sol replied. He just wants to sell newspapers.

Heat climbed my neck like a weed, encircled my throat. What about the Muslim ban? I said. Sol's childhood best friends were Muslim. And wasn't it a Muslim who had risked his life to save Sol when an anti-Semitic mob came calling?

Maybe he'll be good for Israel, Sol said, ignoring me. For the economy. Let's wait and see.

I will recall this conversation after I've waited. After I've seen. I will think of it when Trump separates desperate families at the border, parents and children fleeing persecution; will think of it when Trump falsely claims that Muslims are embedded in a caravan of Central American refugees, stoking nationalistic ire, and when he welcomes to the White House Viktor Orbán, prime minister of Hungary, a man who called Jews dishonorable and lazy and selfish and vengeful, who said Jews "have no homeland, but feel the whole world is theirs."[3] I will think of it when Trump's fear-mongering and foreign policy embolden white supremacists to march in Charlottesville, Virginia, to the tune of "Jews shall not replace us"—and Trump refuses to condemn them. I will think of him when an anti-Semite guns down eleven people at a Shabbat service in Pittsburgh.

But you fled because of intolerance, I persisted. Don't you see that you elected someone who's doing the same thing?

He muttered something in Hebrew. Or maybe it was Arabic. We've been trying and failing to make peace for so long, he said, then petered out. Listen, he said finally. We all have bigotry inside of us. You do too.

Here's what happens when you slip inside someone else's body. When you chant alongside his father on Shabbat. When you eat his mother's lamb pies and pickled peppers. When the glasses out of which he peers get knocked from his face, and his head—your head—is bashed against a wall. Here's what happens when you assume their nation, their faith: Your eyes change. You feel a sudden affinity for the Arabic writing on your neighborhood storefronts. You smile at the Hasidic women pushing strollers past yours on the sidewalk. No one, including you, looks exactly the same.

The poet who narrates Nabokov's "That in Aleppo Once..." marries a woman who doesn't exist. Because she's mythic, he must speak of her, he says, as if she were a character in a story. And yet the woman is so real to him, he is tortured by her memory. How is this possible? Such madness, he fears, is hazardous. If I am not careful, he says, nodding to Othello's suicide, "it may all end in *Aleppo*." Which is to say, he doesn't think he can live inside of a fantasy. Survival—his, yours, ours—depends on truth.

There's a Reuters photo of an al-Qaeda fighter standing erect in an olive grove outside Aleppo. The only skin visible beneath his head-to-toe-black ensemble is around his eyes—dark, with dense brows—and on his hands. One of them grips an assault rifle. All around him and behind him are rows of squat green olive trees. The tip of one skinny branch, a crooked finger, pokes his elbow.

There are no birds—perhaps gunfire scared them off—but if I squint hard enough, I can refashion a speck in the sky into a torso and wings. I want to believe it is Noah's dove, dispatched to see if the earth is drowning or in bloom.

BLACK FOREST

I CAN'T SLEEP. My furnished apartment in Freiburg, Germany, has a TV that broadcasts a single channel, and since I'm too tired to read but too wired to rest, I tune in for half an hour. I speak *nicht Deutch*, just a little Yiddish, but can still make out the tail end of a news program about an Auschwitz survivor, replete with images of rawboned prisoners and the notorious entry gate (WORK SHALL SET YOU FREE); a preview for a film called *Female Agents*, in which lipsticked vixens gun down unsuspecting Nazis; and the start of a sitcom called *Tel Aviv Rendezvous*, in which a guileless guest shows up at a Shabbat dinner with unkosher wine.

It is six hours earlier in New York. I call my husband, tell him about this triad.

What is it? he asks. The atonement channel?

* * *

In the sunniest spot in Germany, clouds roll in, discharge rain, and retreat. It's July, and between short daily storms, the sun blazes. One learns quickly, in the federal state of Baden-Württemberg, to travel with protection: sunscreen and sunglasses. A windbreaker and an umbrella. Shoes that won't get soaked through and subsequently squeak throughout the day.

I have a bag packed with such supplies for my mile-long walk to the University of Freiburg, where I teach an English-language writing seminar, comprising mostly Americans studying abroad. Through the canopy of trees above my head, the sky is intermittently yellow and gray, heartening and menacing. On Günterstalstrasse, the city's main axis, I pass open-faced bakeries, one after the other, whose honey-sweet smell absorbs into my clothes. I am lured in like a bee and promptly order a slice of strawberry-rhubarb pie for breakfast. From my window seat I smile unwittingly at passersby.

The view is aggressively adorable. Trolleys glide along cobblestone streets amid buildings the shade and shape of lemon meringue. Narrow, water-filled canals, vestiges from the Middle Ages, crisscross alleys and abut sidewalks. It seems every window has a box neatly packed with flowers, and everyone, old and young, narrow and wide, rides a bicycle.

I sip espresso and watch folks cluster at the crosswalk. I try not to think about how I jaywalked the day before and an elderly man berated me, all consonants and knitted brows; reproach requires no translation. Nor do I dwell on a German friend's supposition that the man said this: *Ordnung muss sein.* There must be order.

I let a piece of pie dissolve in my mouth and try to decide if it's more sour or sweet. I should do this more, I think: make a meal of dessert. Perhaps I'll start baking in New York, despite my wee galley kitchen and temperamental oven. Even though I don't own proper bakeware. Even though I'm not so good at following directions. Above the rooftops the Black Forest seems to float, a wooded island in the sky.

I never expected my maternal grandmother to sanction my trip to Deutschland. In fact, I held off telling her that I'd accepted a summer teaching post, in part because I didn't want to upset her. Grandma is ninety-two and has a brain tumor. She is prone to passing out. When I finally confessed, a week before leaving—at top volume due to her near-deafness—she barely blinked. I assumed she hadn't heard me.

Germany! I shouted again. Nothing. Had I stunned her into silence? Like so many Jews during the diaspora, my grandmother's family fled pogroms in Eastern Europe and shed their Ashkenazic surname in the States. She and my late grandfather, who helped build our local synagogue, ensured that I was thoroughly versed in our ancestry, in the Holocaust.

I feel guilty, I offered, hoping to diminish her disappointment or assuage a fidgety conscience. Grandma puckered her penciled-on brows and shooed at the air with her hand, as if to say, *Move on.* Then she hunched over a glass and took an uneasy sip of water, a drop of which dribbled down her chin.

* * *

At the University of Freiburg, where philosopher and Nazi Martin Heidegger rose from professor to chair to rector, I meet with students from Pennsylvania and Nebraska and Texas. A few are German. One's from South Africa. All have signed up to learn how to write fiction, to learn about plot and structure and endings and beginnings. We discuss their stories-in-progress, whose subjects vary from loosely true to admittedly contrived: amateur sex, domestic abuse, satanism. They want to master language. (Cue Heidegger: "Man acts as though he were the shaper and master of language, while in fact language remains the master of man.")

The students' drafts are raw and rough. Some are over-dramatic and unconvincing. To the writer of a story with a knife-throwing protagonist, a classmate gripes, That wouldn't happen in real life. Other narratives lack tension. Where's the obstacle? we press. What's at stake?

That afternoon, Nadja, a German student who speaks English, takes the group on a walking tour of Freiburg. She points out popular beer gardens and restaurants and a cinema that shows English-language films for only four euros. She guides us to the Münsterplatz, the center of the city, designed around the mammoth and intricate cathedral. We tip our heads back and marvel. Gothic spires pierce the clouds. Gargoyles poise on the edge of the roof as though bracing to jump.

An art history student notes the statues adorning the facade: prophets, demons, imps. She explains that several of them feature attributes. Like Saint Catherine, virgin princess, gripping the spiked wheel with which she was tortured.

At cafés along the periphery, where diners schmooze under umbrellas, an accordion player pumps vaguely familiar tunes. I can't place them; this nags at me. The sky is graying over. Nearby, a guitarist croons Red Hot Chili Peppers and several students, American and German, chime in. *I don't ever wanna feel like I did that day!* I tongue the salt in my teeth.

When Nadja pauses to plot her next move, I ask if we can go see the synagogue.

The what?

Temple, I offer. House of worship. Church for Jews? I point to the street sign at the corner: PLATZ DER ALTEN SYNAGOGE.

Her face lights up with understanding, as does mine at being understood. Then she shakes her head. The sign, she says, is pointing to where it used to be.

It's a Saturday and cloudless. US-born Emily, who came to Freiburg on a Fulbright, takes me on a hike along the Dreisam River. Locals loll on the banks in the sunshine. Women go topless. Kiddies swim nude. All around us, the forest swells skyward, interrupted only by mounds of vineyards.

Isn't it charming? says Emily. It's not charming. It's Eden. Ducks bob in the current and egrets wade in the shade. Here, she says. She picks a wild raspberry off a vine. Then a blackberry. I swallow. Everything is so goddamn delightful. Isn't there some kind of biblical story like this? A community that's too comfortable, too incautious?

We emerge from a tunnel, on the wall of which someone's graffitied FUCK THE POLICE and into a cloud of white fluff, seeds drifting on the wind.

Emily tells me how the German population is in serious decline, how deaths are outpacing births. There's generous maternity leave, she says, and a new incentive that provides men with a year of paid paternity leave for every child they father.

A year? I shout. Fully paid? She laughs at my enthusiasm. My husband and I want children soon, and our roots are seeking soil. Ever since I'd studied in London for a semester in college, I'd fantasized about moving abroad. Why not Freiburg? Rents are so much cheaper. Health care and education are practically free. Not to mention that the city is eco-friendly even by bohemian Brooklyn standards: vegetation sprouts from rooftops, and solar panels decorate storefronts, and tents are pitched in farmers markets nearly every day. The Green Party has a strong hold here.

I struggle to remember what I even like about New York, consider how I spent the previous year commuting to adjunct teaching gigs in three adjacent states—New Jersey and Connecticut and Pennsylvania—all to rent a Brooklyn apartment with no dishwasher. I assess our wildlife: pigeons and roaches and rats.

In the sunlight, bellies of floating seeds glow like fireflies.

We could hike through the Black Forest every day and bike along the Dreisam. My husband, a runner, would love it.

On a nearby bench, a woman watches us. She is old—older than the war. She has a magazine in her lap, one with articles, I imagine, about motherhood and modern art, one with advertisements for all-natural soap. Church bells echo through the trees. A duck plunges its head in the stream, revealing only its tail and pedaling feet.

Dinner with Emily and her German boyfriend at Oma's Küche, Grandma's Kitchen. I do not think of my own grandma's kosher-style kitchen, which never smelled like this. The menu has a whole page of pork, which I was raised to avoid. I feast instead on spinach-and-cheese-filled crepes and buttery white wine from a local vineyard (all listed in English! I don't even need to know German to get by!). Afterward we wind our way through the university square, past a clock tower and a Starbucks and a jewelry store with precious stones twinkling just out of reach. It's the weekend of the Schlossbergfest music festival, and as I climb a hill toward the edge of the forest, I bump into a few of my students buying shots from a veil-wearing bride-to-be: a tradition, Emily says, that helps new couples pay for their wedding. The undergraduates love it here.

What's not to love? I say.

The festival is packed. Locals and tourists and teenagers and retirees crowd around performances and beer stands, clapping and smoking and shouting. We push our way toward a paved pathway that takes us to a slightly less congested section in the back. On stage, Van Halen lookalikes croon Pink Floyd's "Comfortably Numb." Someone says, Germans love American rock. I seek out beer, and though I can't understand what the vendor says through his discolored teeth, I pretend I do. The stein is twice the size of a stateside mug, and I walk extra slowly, waves of foam cresting the edge.

So cheap, I say.

No, says a friend, you got the cute-girl discount. When I turn around, the vendor is giving me a hyperbolic thumbs-up. *Prost!* It's too dark for anyone to see me blush.

I am equally ashamed and proud to know every song the German Van Halen covers. Aerosmith and the Eagles and Creedence Clearwater Revival. After a second stein, I am singing aloud. Everyone is giddy by the time we tumble down the mountainside and into the desolate residential streets, where we bid one another *auf wiedersehen*. Is it the New Yorker in me that feels threatened by the dark or is it my unquenchable anxiety? The forest is my guide. If I keep it to my right, I'll eventually reach home. Under the full moon, the canopy is impenetrably black and my shadow overtakes the sidewalk. I note how the air tastes purer and more oxygenated than it does at home, how I'm so used to inhaling exhaust fumes, how this town is inconceivably quiet—no sirens!—how I could live here; I could totally live here; why couldn't I live here?; how I could write and teach and grow tomatoes and get a dog—two dogs!—and send my kids to the international school and there's something shiny on the pavement, something glowing, and when I bend down, I see it's a cobblestone-sized plaque, a brass "stumbling block" at the base of a residential driveway.

HERE LIVED ROBERT GRUMBACH. BORN 1875, arrested, deported to Dachau, then to Gurs. Beside it is a brass plaque for his wife. HIER WOHNTE BERTA GRUMBACH.

I'd read that some residents in victims' homes protested the installment of these *Stolpersteine* when a German artist first proposed the project, in the 1990s. The value of their property would depreciate, they said. And who wants to be reminded of the genocide every time you go in and out of your house? It wasn't the current tenants' fault that certain groups were scapegoated. That the Grumbachs disappeared.

Beyond the metal gate safeguarding the property, two Volkswagens sit head to toe. There's a figure watching me from an upstairs window. Or maybe it's just a curtain shifting in the breeze. I rub my heel on the brass to shine it and feel a prickle of impending weather, moisture in the air. I sprint the rest of the way home, arrive winded. In the morning, the streets are dry.

BOY IN BLUE

MOST MORNINGS, MY FOUR-YEAR-OLD arrests me. Usually he's in uniform, a blue jacket with yellow buttons and a matching peaked cap.

I saw you stealing, he'll say, nose crumpled like he smells trash. He yanks toy handcuffs out of his pocket and jiggles them. You're going to jail.

The narrative plays out a number of ways depending on how much coffee I've had, how committed I am to role-playing at 7 a.m.

For how long? I might say.

Five minutes, he'll reply, or else something more cryptic and unsettling: nineteen.

Nineteen what?

I resist, say, It wasn't me, Officer. You're mistaken!

Sometimes his brother, Oliver, age six, is my alibi. *It wasn't Mommy!*

Officer Leo squints, shifts his lower jaw from side to side, mumbles something to headquarters on his faux walkie-talkie. His superiors are surprisingly flexible.

I'm sorry, ma'am, he says finally, and unfastens my binds. *It wasn't you. It was someone who looked like you.*

Which is to say, a woman whom the world sees as white.

I ascribe Leo's fixation to geography. We live two doors down from a New York City precinct station. Before we moved in, my thoughts on the apartment's location were comprehensible. I disliked how the huge municipal building sapped the block of charm. Wondered if we'd be less likely to have our bikes stolen off our front patio? (Nope.) If we'd have ready access to help? (Yep; officers have twice given our dead car engine a jump.) What I didn't account for were the effects of my sons' exposure to law enforcement. How after a Minneapolis police officer killed George Floyd by kneeling on his neck, our block would be cordoned off for weeks to prevent citizens from demonstrating their rightful outrage, and come nightfall would serve as a headquarters for state police and ICE officers in combat gear. I didn't consider that a dozen times a day, all year long, we'd walk past men and women in uniform on our shared sidewalk. Sometimes they're in bulletproof vests. Sometimes they're gathered ceremoniously on the precinct steps.

Sometimes they're leading a person in handcuffs out of the backseat of a cruiser and across our path into the station. My children study their equipment belts, which are at their eye level, look back and forth between the arrestee and the officers clutching their elbows.

Leo will want to know things when we get home. What the bad guy did. (I'm not sure.) How the officers caught him. (I don't know.) If the handcuffs lock, since his do not, and what kind of food they serve in jail, and if the person will be imprisoned for one or eleven days and what do the officers do if he escapes? Leo will want me to know that when he's a cop, he will be the best bad-guy-getter in Brooklyn. My toes curl. I will wonder, What would he dress like if we lived on a different block? In a different city? In a different country?

Sometimes I push other outfits. Want to be a superhero today? I say. Or a sea creature? I dig out a squid hat.

My suggestions confuse him. No, he says, clipping a ring of keys onto his belt loop. I told you, I want to be an officer. Also, he says, he's missing something that all real officers have. A gun. Can't he get a toy one?

Dramatic play, experts say, can help children sort out fantasy from reality. Can help them learn about symbols. What, I'd like to know, does a lethal weapon symbolize?

* * *

One morning, while Officer Leo patrols the living room, Oliver sidles up to me in his pajamas. He is quiet, checking to see if any of his teeth are loose, eager to have a jack-o'-lantern mouth like the other kids in second grade. He's one of the youngest in his class. Nothing moves. He sighs, starts to speak, stops.

Most people we see in handcuffs, he says, have brown skin. He holds my gaze, scans it for something. Opinion. Emotion. He wants to know what this means, how to feel about it.

They do, I say, gut seizing. I sustain wide eye contact, an attempt to buy time. I think, This is how the association coalesces: the good/bad with the cop/criminal with the white/brown.

I mutter something about how Black and Latinx folks make up less than a third of the population but more than half of those imprisoned. That criminality and law enforcement are complicated, that people with white skin break just as many laws. Everything feels inadequate. Opaque.

Oliver sucks his thumb.

Sometimes, I say, officers make mistakes.

This is also not an answer. Systemic racism is not a mistake. Nor is an inequitable status quo that officers must uphold. Where to begin? What's the beginning?

I say, Someone can make a bad choice, and it doesn't mean they're a bad guy. I do not know if I am talking about the arrestee or the officer. What's a good guy?

I say, Not all people are treated equally.

* * *

A Saturday. Leo stares into his bowl of Cheerios as if decoding a pattern. The visor of his police hat obscures his face. Behind us, Oliver plays with LEGOs: good guys versus bad guys.

Where do officers bring criminals, Leo asks, if the prison is full?

That's a problem, I say. America has too many prisoners.

He chews, frowns. Last week, he wanted to know what America was. It's a country, I said, a big piece of land.

But what *is* it? he asked. He did not understand the profundity of his question. Did not know it stoked in me notions of nationalism and sameness and difference, conjured the current president's solution to making America "great": giant, xenophobic walls at the country's borders. That America, to Donald Trump and so many politicians alongside him and before him, is a place for people who look like he does. A place for people who look like my sons.

I say, America has way more prisoners than any other country, and it's not because people here behave extra badly. There are whole schools of people in lockup, I say. Entire cities. Maybe, I say, too many things count as crimes?

He nods.

Maybe, I say, there's a better solution than prison when people don't follow the little rules?

Leo wipes his milk mustache with his uniform sleeve. Then he hops off the counter stool. I wonder if he's going to shed his costume and rejoin the civilian population of his family. I want him to say, *The only fight worth having is one for civil rights!* Instead, he cuffs me.

You're unarrested, he says, his misunderstanding of under arrest.

In my bedroom, a.k.a. the precinct station, he tells me to have a seat. The stock narrative resumes.

I saw you stealing, he says, voice rugged with faux fury. Why did you steal?

I'm sorry, Officer, I say. I lost my job and my children were hungry. I needed money to feed them.

He is quiet. Unmoved by my oversimplification, maybe. Your kids are hungry? he says.

I nod.

Why didn't you just ask me for money?

You?

Yes! I have tons of money. I'm a *police officer*. Here, take some. He puts his hand in mine. Invisible currency. Take it, he says. You're free to go.

What I say when my four-year-old asks if I've ever been arrested for real: Yes.

What did you do? he asks.

I say I stole clothes. That I was sixteen and made a hare-brained decision. That I didn't want to spend my babysitting money. That I wanted to get merchandise for free.

I don't say that I also wanted to impress two blonder, cooler high school classmates with whom I was vacationing in Vermont, girls who flicked price tags off blazers as effortlessly as they flipped their hair. That I developed a fail-safe plan to carry an armload of clothes out the store's front door because who would suspect such a brazen move? I'd be hidden in plain sight.

Leo asks what happened next.

I got caught, I say.

Handcuffed?

I nod, say there were witnesses, that a cashier called the cops.

I don't say that fifteen minutes into our escape, Ace of Base blasting from the car stereo, a corporal in a wide-brimmed hat pulled us over on the interstate, that I sobbed and begged while he summoned me out of the backseat and cuffed me against the trunk, that I was taken to the station and fingerprinted and mug-shot, that panic crept into my lungs and capillaries and my nose bled all over my shirt. That my biggest concern was not getting punished or hurt or killed, but not getting into college.

Did you go to jail? Leo asks. Did you escape?

How to explain that I was promptly released, despite committing felony retail theft, a charge determined by the value of the merchandise ($196 in 1994)? That the corporal said he could tell I came from a "good" family? That he recommended the district attorney consider me for a first-time offenders' program, and that the program for felons cost $100, which we could afford? That the program required that I purchase $196 of clothing for a teen in foster care, which we could also afford? That I listed the dozens of hours of requisite volunteer work on my college applications under "extracurricular activities"—the same application on which I checked the box saying no, I'd never been convicted of a crime? Because there was no crime? Because my criminal record had been expunged? How to explain that I got into the Ivy League college of my choice?

A playdate at our place. The other boy's mom lingers at drop-off, wanting to make sure her son is comfortable. We hardly know each other. She scans our apartment.

I have a few errands to run, she says, and then I'll be back.

No worries, I say. Leo already has his arms full of cop costume.

Dramatic play, experts say, can help with a child's social interaction skills.

My mom was arrested, he announces. She broke the law.

The other mom lifts her eyebrows, grins at me with uncertain teeth.

Shoplifting, I say. High school.

She laughs. I laugh.

This will be Leo's broadcast for weeks. He will tell my in-laws, and my colleagues who come over for dinner, and the plumber who attempts to wrench out a toothbrush that's been flushed down the toilet. Is it a novelty just because I'm his mom? Clearly he doesn't know what to make of this information. I watch him say it aloud—Police put her in handcuffs—watch him gauge others' reactions and, by turn, modulate his own. I wonder if I confessed too soon.

* * *

One weekend morning in March, fourteen months before the murder of George Floyd, Leo declares that he wants to report for duty. Maybe he's sick of arresting his parents. Maybe he wants to be among his own kind. He's already in uniform.

You want to go to the precinct? I ask.

He nods, says, The real one.

I hem and haw and acquiesce. He adjusts the ID card on which he's scrawled "LEO" in blue ink and which he's clipped to his chest. Together we march next door, past the line of patrol cars and up the steps and through the double doors. Leo pauses in the entryway, hands on hips, either waiting to be noticed or suddenly intimidated by his fantasy-turned-reality. Perhaps a bit of both. Behind a large elevated desk along the right-hand wall, two cops are chatting. No one looks up. The vending machines buzz.

I say, Officer Leo, reporting for duty!

A Latinx woman in uniform approaches, bends over, shakes his hand. She admires his tools. You have a whistle, she says, and a radio! She taps his walkie-talkie. Lets him hold her handcuffs. I wonder what it's like to be a woman on the force.

What else do you have? Leo asks, eyeing all the bulges in her duty belt. What's that?

Pepper spray, she says, rubbing the black leather lump with a manicured hand. We spray it in the bad guys' eyes.

Leo's pupils enlarge. He's not heard of such a thing. Later, he'll want to know why he doesn't have pepper spray.

His eyes flick to her holster. I half wait for him to ask her if he can touch it, half fear she will agree. Why do you have a gun? he asks.

She pats the grip, says, In case the bad guy has a gun.

I hear Wayne LaPierre's voice—and that of every other NRA apologist—emerge from her mouth. I detest that she's armed. I detest more that she has to be. Doesn't she?

Leo follows the officer into a side room with two empty holding cells. The air smells rank. Body odor, maybe. Mildew.

Want to see where we put the bad guys? she says.

The holding cells are empty. On a future visit, they won't be. On a future visit, as Leo struts through the precinct like a captain, all long strides and stiff arms, I will notice a thin man with dark hair in the cell. Leo will have trouble averting his eyes. I will yank his wrist, tell him that it's impolite to stare. Instead he will be ushered to the center of the precinct, where an officer will flank him and call to me—Take a photo, Mom!—and behind my wide-smiling son, through the glass, the man will have his head in his hands, and my mouth will go dry.

Today, though, nobody's caged. The officer tugs one of the heavy doors, ushers Leo inside, pulls it shut.

Whaddya think? she says.

He grips the metal bars, peers out, awestruck. A cop in the clink.

I want to tell my sons about the extreme rarity of police convictions,[4] even amid video evidence of guilt. How there's still no singular, legal definition of *excessive force*. How officers are three times more likely to kill Black people than white people,[5] even though white people are more likely to be armed,[6] a reality that America's chief law enforcement officer, Bill Barr, blames on "a few bad apples."[7] How Trump has made armored vehicles and grenade launchers and bayonets accessible to police.[8] I want to explain machismo, how domestic abuse is more common among law enforcement officers than NFL players,[9] how battering a spouse seldom results in punishment, let alone a lost job. At the same time, I don't want to taint their opinion of the officers we see daily, the ones who have been kind to us, who, when a coronavirus demands that New Yorkers shelter in place, still answer 911 calls and put themselves at risk. I don't want my kids to generalize, to make personal an issue that's institutional. So I do what I often do when unsure of something. I read.

Where to begin? What's the beginning?

I look up the history of policing in America, learn that our first official force was established in Boston in 1838, something I vaguely knew.[10] I also discover something I didn't know, but that shouldn't have surprised me: that modern policing grew out of practices established in the Colonial South. There, the aim was not to catch criminals but to oppress slaves.[11] As far back as the early 1700s, a legally sanctioned, organized network of "patrollers" surveilled their assigned "beats" to apprehend runaways, terrorize workers, and prevent revolts. Slave patrols typically comprised white men on horseback armed with whips, guns, and ropes.[12]

Sometimes when Leo walks around our Brooklyn neighborhood in uniform, he earns greetings from passersby—*What up, Chief!*—that seem to surprise him. It's as if his persona resides so deeply in his imagination that he forgets others can see it too. There's a fume in the air after these comments, one that's almost too subtle to notice: the heraldry of dominance and toughness that my boys can't help but inhale.

Leo twirls a whistle on a rope, says, Mom, see any crooks?

I remind him that his job is not just to catch criminals but to help people. Someone might be lost, I say, or need assistance crossing the street. Leo entertains this—Maybe their cat ran away?—but not for long. The oppositional narrative, the binary, is much more exciting.

Let me know if you spot anyone suspicious, he says.

It is a privilege, I think, that he wants to play Officer Leo, a privilege that he still associates the uniform with undiluted goodness because he's never been warned otherwise, never been told to take precautions to protect himself. A privilege, and a concern, that his small, white body so easily inhabits the role.

My Bronx-born father was a police officer, or at least he played one in the 1980s. For a few years in my early childhood, Dad joined the auxiliary force as a part-time volunteer. We had moved to a new town in Westchester County, New York, adjacent to where he taught public elementary school, and he wanted to connect to the community. To help out, he said. Make friends. After a brief training course, the particulars of which he can't recall, he received an official uniform, one indistinct from that of professional officers. I have fleeting memories of him walking through the kitchen wearing it, then trundling down to the basement.

Dad welcomed the menial assignments, like supervising church crossings and redirecting traffic. He's still proud of his scheme the evening before Halloween, a.k.a. "mischief night." How he stationed himself at the supermarket's exit and intercepted reams of unsuspecting teenage boys. How he seized dozens of cartons of eggs (*Were they all making omelets?*) and cans of shaving cream (*Their faces had no hair!*).

But he was also assigned the kind of work for which he needed to complete a firearms training course and carry a gun. He performed after-hours "door checks" of local businesses and patrolled neighborhoods after dark. He didn't like the gun part, which I knew, but felt reassured to hear. (Dad and I don't always see eye to eye on politics.) I asked him why not.

How many times have you gotten into an argument and said things you'll regret? he says. Can you imagine a hothead with a weapon?

Leo points a stick at me, cocks his head as if aiming.

Put that down, I say.

He fires anyway. He has been doing this a lot lately, making guns with branches and LEGOs and his fingers, incorporating them into games. I denied his request for a police gun, repeating what I said to his appeal for a Nerf Blaster and X-Shot Water Warfare Pressure Jet: real guns hurt people; I don't think it's fun to pretend to hurt people; there are more firearms than people in the US;[13] one hundred people die in our country from guns every single day.[14]

Put that down, I shout. My firearms kibosh is failing. Making them more desirable, the way my parents' television embargo made me salivate at the sight of one. It is not that I think Nerf guns are a gateway to violence. It is more that I can't abide the sight of them. I am too enraged, too upset. In our house, I think, there will be gun control.

Officer Leo wants to know what to do if the bad guy has a gun. What then?

I say, Call for backup.

But the police officer said—

Listen to your mother.

Dad didn't like that he had to go to so many meetings as a squad member, a chore he already felt burdened by as an educator. The last one he attended before he quit the corps was for all the professional and auxiliary officers in the area. The topic? The use of force. Dad recalls a high-ranking official explaining the Constitution and applicable laws, clarifying citizens' rights, insisting that officers not use their weapons unless their lives were in imminent danger.

Of course, the officer said, if the suspect is a scumbag, be rough. The room snickered.

And if the suspect is an asshole, he said, be rougher.

Laughter.

Just be careful, the officer said, because you don't want to turn the scumbag into an asshole.

You know, says Dad, that was thirty-five years ago. A different time. Things have changed.

The Fraternal Order of Police, ostensibly the largest police union in the world, endorsed Donald Trump for president in 2016. Trump, they said, "understands and supports our priorities, and our members believe he will make America safe again."[15]

A year later, in July 2017, President Trump gave a speech to a large law enforcement crowd in Long Island, not far from where I live with my children. He lamented the mistreatment of police, decried how for years, laws have protected criminals instead of officers.

"If you do something wrong, you're in more jeopardy than they are," Trump said. "These laws are stacked against you." When apprehending people, Trump told the cops, "please don't be too nice."[16]

According to the experts, dramatic play lets children helpfully imitate what they see and hear. You may catch words, say the experts, that your children have picked up from you or their teachers or others in charge.

Leo is making pepper spray from a toilet paper roll. Can I help him cut out cardboard circles for the top and bottom? he asks. Color his creation with a black Sharpie so it looks like the real thing?

I take a deep breath, hold steady. Why don't we try something that doesn't hurt people's bodies? I say.

He whines, stamps his feet, then stops. An idea. What about a dog? he says. He has seen them, the police dogs. Their heft. Their teeth.

I guess? I say. At least nobody will go temporarily blind?

He ties a rope around the neck of a stuffed animal, pulls it around the living room, pats its head. Then he spots an outlaw. His brother.

Doggie, he shouts, attack!

Was it obvious? It wasn't to me, not for a while. How Leo's the youngest, the least in charge, the most defiant, the most likely to wind up in time out; how he needs to dramatize the rules and consequences of life in a way that his milder-mannered older brother, who has no interest in officering, never did. In a way the other costumes in his dress-up bin—doctor, polar bear, astronaut—don't permit. In a way that his parents' professional roles—college professor and nonprofit executive—don't encourage, either.

Dramatic play, experts say, can offer a child relief from emotional tension.

How eager Leo is to be an authority instead of an underling, I think now. How helpful it is that play lets him say and do things that he cannot express otherwise, to work out the anxieties endemic to littleness. It's not that Leo necessarily wants to be a cop. Leo, I think, wants power.

What else wasn't obvious: that that's what I want too. When I see Leo jiggle handcuffs and aim his finger gun, I feel a surge of helplessness. What these tools symbolize to me is all that my sons will assimilate before my husband and I can run proper interference and how long we will have to wait to thoroughly explain privilege and history and brutality and misogyny and the racism that lives in them, that lives in us, the kind we inherit without knowing it, the damage we do without meaning to. How large is the gulf, I want to know, between what a parent knows and what a child cannot understand? How vast is the harm society will do to my sons and the harm they will inevitably do in return while their mother waits for them to grow up?

At five, Leo will still have a post in law enforcement, will hide handcuffs and a badge in his kindergarten backpack because, he'll say, he's undercover. Teachers will refer to him as "sheriff," a nickname he'll wear like a badge of honor.

Just after his sixth birthday, in May 2020, the uniform largely forgotten in its bin, Leo will join me in squeezing past the barrier and the row of officers at the end of our block to accompany hundreds of protesters gathered on the other side. He will hold a Black Lives Matter sign high above his head while seated on my husband's shoulders and participate in chants decrying police brutality. For days he will repeat what he's heard us say in response to a sign in a window across the street: that *all lives won't matter until Black lives matter.* At the same time, his comprehension half-baked, he will build jail cells and police cars out of LEGOs nearly every afternoon.

My son still misunderstands what officers say when taking people into custody.

You're unarrested, the LEGO officer in his left hand says to a LEGO wrongdoer in his right. You were speeding; you were robbing; you hurt someone; I saw you.

Dramatic play, experts say, helps children understand the power of language.

We've yet to correct him. In Leo's linguistic reality, freedom rules. Nobody suffers. Everyone is equal. Everyone is blameless.

ULTRA SOUND

MY MOTHER IS ONSTAGE at the Night Owl Café in Greenwich Village. It's 1966. Floppy-haired, bell-bottomed men surround her, one of whom is Ron, the boyfriend she'll harmonize with for years until he breaks her heart. There's a spotlight on her face and she is ethereal: middle-parted hair to her ribs, head tilted, mouth open. She looks impassioned. Self-possessed. The men grip guitar necks and drumsticks, but she is the one in the light. She is the one to behold. My mother is singing—belting, even.

But it is only a photo, and I cannot hear her.

I do not say this to Dee.

Dee: my mother's childhood friend and my sole contact in Tucson, Arizona, where I've just moved for graduate school. It's August 2004. Dee snapped the photo at the Night Owl nearly four decades before and has retrieved it from one of her meticulously organized albums. In the low-ceilinged living room of her adobe home, we consider it.

Gorgeous, right? she says, scooching closer to me on the couch. You both are. You could be twins. She fiddles with her waist-long gray braid.

I uncross my legs, thighs slick with sweat. It is ninety-eight degrees outside, blood hot, and only marginally cooler under Dee's fan. Around us, life hums: Her Yorkshire terriers scratch and yip at our feet. A cockatoo squawks from a cage by the kitchen. I hold the print by its edges as my mother's taught me to—*Oil from fingers can make a memory fade*—and feel Dee's smile recede like an inhalation. She misses my pre-mother mother, I think, or the fervor of their friendship, one that peaked in youth and dwindled with distance and time and human transmutation. I imagine she's burrowing through memory holes, hopping among basket houses on MacDougal Street, grooving with the crowd. It's easy to envision Dee among beatniks. Dee, with her flowy garb and jangly earrings and braids. Unlike my mother, she still looks the part.

I'd met Dee as a preteen when she visited New York, watched her age in the photo postcards she sent each New Year. She was the woman my mother periodically disappeared to visit. The girl in the stories of Mom's wayward high school days in suburban New York. The two of them met in French class in 1960. They were like-minded artists, nonconformists, conscientious objectors to pressure and expectation. They had complicated home lives. They have the same unapologetic laugh.

Dee got pregnant at nineteen, way before my mother warmed to motherhood, and left town with Lloyd, to whom she's still married. My mother dropped out of college in New York to join Ron's band.

She pats her lap and a small brown dog jumps into it, twirls, settles. Dee strokes its head, asks about my boyfriend in New York. I tell her that he's a musician. I tell her that he's met my mother.

Your mother, she says, shaking her head. It is hard to decode her tone. Amusement or exasperation or nostalgia or all three or something else entirely. Maybe she assumes I know what the proclamation implies so she doesn't have to elaborate. Or maybe she doesn't say more because my mother's a jumble of thoughts and feelings and Dee can't parse them. Neither can I.

I shake my head too. *My mother.*

What I know about Mom's musical past at this point is optical. Static. Derived from a wall of fame in our childhood den. A glossy press shot of her first folk-rock group, the Ragamuffins. A clipping of her face from the *Village Voice* promoting an upcoming tour. A framed album cover from 1971: her and Ron's solemn mugs atop a cartoon landscape of rolling hills and lollipop trees. *Billboard* magazine would name it a "Special Merit Pick" alongside an album by Cat Stevens.

There were also the stories she proffered sporadically, usually sparked by a song on the radio, stories that seemed as fantastic and improbable as dreams. About how she shared a stage with Van Morrison. Jammed with James Taylor. Opened for the Doors. How Jim Morrison borrowed her tambourine and threw it out into the crowd in an exuberant fit. How someone somewhere probably has a 1969 Doors instrument that actually belongs to her.

As a teenager, I told these tales at parties. They impressed people. Which made me seem impressive. This was the 1990s, the heyday of a new generation of fans of sixties music, the same stretch in which I dressed as a hippie for successive Halloweens because there was a garbage bag in the attic full of her stage frocks—flowery bell-bottoms and fur-lined coats and royal purple sheaths. My long, straight hair naturally parted in the middle. I was slim like her too. When I'd emerge from the bathroom in costume, Mom would squeal, redden, cover her mouth.

I can't stand it, she'd say.

There was also a story so momentous that friends of friends knew of me because of it. Proof lived on our den wall: an enlarged snapshot of my mother with Jimi Hendrix, known then as Jimmy James. He has a bandanna tied around his head, a scanty moustache above his toothy grin, an arm draped over her shoulder. My mother's bright, youthful face is caught in mid-laugh. Tucked into the corner of the frame is his handwritten note: "I still love you and I always will."

Jimi proposed, Mom would say. It was 1966 and he'd just been discovered on the same stage where her band had a regular gig. He was headed to England, where he'd gain fame, where he'd later die, and urged her to join him. My mother demurred. She loved Ron, she'd say. Not to mention that Jimi was high all the time.

The picture had mythical status among a few classmates. Stoners, mostly. A few times they came over just to squint at Jimi's scrawl and the sloppy hearts he'd sketched around my mother's name. You could've been Courtney Hendrix, they'd say, then run their eyes over me as if scrutinizing the pigment of my skin. As if maybe I wasn't telling them everything. As if maybe my mother hadn't told me everything. Maybe I was half-Hendrix.

I didn't tell people that I knew only the star part of Mom's rock stardom, that I'd never heard her songs. By high school, this had begun to gnaw at me.

I have to find the records, she'd say when I asked, though I could tell from the lull between words and the way her eyes shifted that she wouldn't look for them, that they probably weren't even lost. This was pre-internet. I'd wait a few months and try again. I sounded awful, Mom would say. I promised her she wasn't as bad as she thought, but her expression darkened. Why do you care?

My motivations were complex. I'd developed an interest in the arts by then, intrigued by how color could evoke mood, how metaphors could shift vantage points. I was learning that art was a language, and I wanted to hear her communicate. This is because my mother is enigmatic. Private. Struggles to articulate thoughts and feelings, so rarely does. As a kid, I wanted things from her I couldn't name. Not just affection—though I wanted that too. I wanted more of her.

Leave it, she'd say, when I pressed.

How to read such caginess? And what to make of my mammoth need? Why did it seem like I pursued this harder than my older sister, my younger brother? My mother told me she loved me. Did I doubt her? Some things were hard to reconcile. Like the construction project my parents undertook when I was seven, building a bedroom just for her, separate from my father—he snored, she said, made sleep impossible. Her new twin bed inhibited snuggling. Or how, despite his multiple jobs, my dad was the designated "night man": if my siblings or I was sick or scared in the night and went to her, she dispatched us to him. Or her vague answers to all manner of questions, and the live-in caregiver we had even as she stayed at home. Her love was hard to perceive. Perhaps, I thought, this was because she was hard to perceive. A paint-by-number profile with only some sections filled in. A stroke of jaw. A cluster of ribs. A clavicle. I was missing segments. I was missing colors.

Somewhere in our attic or one of our house's many locked closets, a piece of her was etched into vinyl, preserved in concentric grooves. I just didn't know where to look.

Absent access, I set out to compose her rock persona. As an undergrad, I enrolled in History of the 1960s for contextual clues, even found references to her and Ron in a library book.

In graduate school in Baltimore, a program I completed pre-Tucson, I submitted an essay about her short-lived career that I'd written by hand in the middle of the night.

On a weekend getaway to Woodstock, New York, where shops peddled posters of her former friends, nearly all of them dead, I looked for her in the record bins.

I looked for Ron too. Ron, consistent collaborator, living witness, a man whose face on our den wall my eyes had assimilated, along with relatives' faces, assuring his place in my mental family tree. As the internet populated, I traced his path from Greenwich Village to the Catskills to Europe and back again. I knew only bits about Ron from my mother, glass beads I'd acquired across years and strung together. That he was part-Portuguese. That he'd avoided the draft because of flat feet. That he was a prick.

Dee offers to show me her studio. I trail her down the hall to a spacious, light-filled room teeming with works-in-progress and looms that are as large as harpsichords. I want to strum them. She shares information with an ease that moves me: what she's working on, what she wants to try next, how she relies on technology to transpose images onto fabric. She shows me a recent creation, a tapestry of graphic faces with their tongues entwined. It's the kind of zany and subversive aesthetic my mother shares, and that I appreciate.

Outside the window, sun glints off heaps of metal.

Lloyd's studio is out front, she says, if you want to see it.

I snicker, say, Hard to miss. Her husband, Lloyd, a steel sculptor, transformed their yard into a metallic jungle so fantastical that it's a tourist destination. I had navigated it on my walk to their front door, crouching to pet spring-bodied dogs, dodging overhead birds with trowel wings, pausing at his workstation to laugh at a bucktoothed beast with a faucet penis.

My mother's a visual artist, too, hardwired to see compositions and designs and symbolism everywhere. In my childhood she channeled ideas into jewelry—inventive, whimsical, one-of-a-kind necklaces and brooches and rings she made for herself and wore with pride. When I asked, in middle school, why she didn't sell or display her work, she crossed her arms, said someone might steal her ideas or take advantage. It happens all the time, she would say.

Dee tells me how she and Lloyd regularly open their home for arts-and-culture tours. I think about Mom's studio, the one we tacked onto the back of the house at the same time we built her bedroom. I think about how its door was permanently locked. How Mom covered the door's glass panels with tinfoil.

What she said: I have expensive equipment.

What she said: My work is no one's business.

What I heard: *Art is a secret.*

*   *   *

I moved to Tucson from Baltimore after completing a yearlong master of arts program, one that instead of conferring mastery exposed how little I knew about craft. My admission to Johns Hopkins' top-ranked Writing Seminars had been something of a fluke: I'd submitted a rant from my journal, and an unorthodox professor mistook the work for informed experimentation. Once enrolled, I couldn't replicate what I'd done, nor could I explain why it had satisfied. I spent the next six months working backward, taking stories apart, sorting out mechanics. The process was deflating. Painful.

I could've quit. Chased something else. Several people from our twelve-person program did, or at least procured new roles thereafter: celebrity journalist, critical theorist, high school teacher, policy wonk. But writing had seized me. I couldn't shake it.

I wrote—I write—because I prize language's surprises and limitations, and because in college I connected to books more than I did to friends. Literature offered throughways to comprehension, to compassion, to a quieter mind. Writing offered the same, though its lens flipped around, allowed me to introspect, test assumptions, unscramble experiences and observations. It was an attempt to participate in the conversation rather than just nod along to it.

That's why I'd applied for an MFA, to attain the so-called terminal degree in creative writing. Why I accepted a fellowship at the University of Arizona—two years of subsidized focus—and moved to the desert, even though my boyfriend was tethered to the East Coast. Even though my friends were climbing their respective career ladders and getting married and having kids. I couldn't quit any more than I could fret over my mother having done just that.

Mom says she watched Janis Joplin, in a nightclub bathroom, slathering so much cover-up on her face you could hardly see her skin. That she chatted with a dishwasher named Joe Cocker. Played drums for Arlo Guthrie while he worked on "Alice's Restaurant." I exhumed more on an internet deep-dive. An ad for her and Ron's performance at Madison Square Garden with Sly and the Family Stone. A note about how she and Ron were slated to perform on *The Tonight Show Starring Johnny Carson* and would have, had their group not disbanded.

I also found interviews with Ron. In one online article, Ron described his friendship with Jimi Hendrix, claimed Jimi used Ron's matches to light up his guitar onstage at the Monterey International Pop Festival, in California, in a now-epic performance.

The time I burned my guitar, it was like a sacrifice, Jimi would say later. You sacrifice the things you love.

Ron explained how Jimi had passed through New York before he went to the festival. The men had shared a smoke.

I sourced video footage of the performance in an attempt to triangulate my links to both men. I feel an unearned fondness for Jimi, who died eight years before I took a breath. His two-dimensional likeness had kept me company in our den until I left for college. I still simper when I see his face on T-shirts or hear his songs on the radio, wistful for an experience I never had, for a time I never lived. *You could've been Courtney Hendrix.*

Jimi had been in his element in Monterey, all ruffles and primary colors, wailing "Wild Thing" into the mic, creating ear-splitting feedback with his Stratocaster, dropping to his knees to hump it and kiss its strings. He retrieved lighter fluid and sprayed a stream from just below his belt, and the moment he lifted a match, I pressed PAUSE. The matchbook was a blurry white square, discarded in half a second. Impossible to decode. Ron hadn't even been at the festival; he and my Mom stayed behind in Greenwich Village. Is a matchbook the kind of detail Jimi would've mentioned to Ron afterward? Had I caught my mother's ex in a lie?

Jimi summoned the fire with his fingers and the flames obliged, leaping and twirling, a performance of their own, and then Jimi grabbed his instrument and smashed it against the stage floor.

Recently I unearthed a half-page Columbia Records ad in a 1971 issue of *Circus* magazine that features a photo of the two of them. Ron is seated, their album propped against his knee. My mother peeks over his shoulder, a disembodied head.

Ron and my mom "are an efficient team," reads the text

beside them. "He is in a world of creating full songs from an inspired note or two, all through the night. She wakes to new songs each morning." Her role on this team, her contribution, according to the ad, is that she "remembers" songs that Ron forgets and reminds him.

Ron's work was derivative, Mom says. She was writing music, too, and he liked it—just not as much as he liked his own.

In Fiction Workshop, core class of the MFA program, we aspiring writers mine our lives. There is a story about coffin shopping, by an Arizonan who buried a parent. A story of teenage widowhood in an Indian village, written by a classmate whose grandmother suffered such a fate. A story of racial terrorism, written by a Southern activist. I assign characters my own preoccupations: love and faith and mental illness. Also, always, motherhood. My protagonists are aspiring mothers and new mothers and daughters struggling to get close to their mothers. The fixation's tied to my own hopes that I'll eventually be a mother—I have newly pregnant friends—but it is also an effort to fathom this singular and labyrinthine relationship with the most insistent tool I have: storytelling.

I don't know what prompts Dee's next question. Maybe there isn't a prompt. Maybe it's just that my mother is an invisible presence in the room and Dee can make her manifest. All I can say is that she poses it casually. We are back on her cushy living room couch by then. I have a Yorkshire terrier in my lap and am giggling over a Bible from her bookshelf whose pages are fastened together with a giant bolt.

Want to listen to your mother's music? she says.

I must look shocked.

What? she says, laughing. What!

Books and articles don't contain my mother's personal stories, ones I learned in dribs and drabs and never felt comfortable raising with my grandparents during their lifetimes. My grandmother snubbed her albums, Mom says, wouldn't listen to them. My grandfather, a cerebral CEO, thought she was a dilettante. On one rare visit to her parents' home in suburban New York, an hour from her and Ron's apartment, she discovered her vinyl record in pieces on her childhood bed and left in tears.

This last bit she shared with me over the phone when I was in Baltimore, and I saw her face even though she was hundreds of miles away: the overcast eyes and slack cheeks. I tried to imagine being renounced for pursuing writing. How lonesome it must have felt. How distressing. I tried to imagine the end of her musical career, too, something else absent from public record, something that resulted in her moving back in with those same parents. All that work and promise reduced to half a sentence in someone else's bio. When "Ron's album" with my mother didn't succeed, according to an article in *FolkWax*, "the duo drifted apart."

My mother has a different account. It doesn't involve drifting. It involves a breach.

I dare say that after seven years and three albums together—after living in the notoriously cruddy Hotel Albert, in Greenwich Village; after singing all night and sleeping all day and wandering through Washington Square Park, only to look up at the leafless trees and realize she had missed all of autumn; after her father drove up to a club and urged her to finish college and she refused; after she came home to find Ron in their bed with another woman, and learned there had been others—the earth opened beneath her feet.

Dee retrieves the 1971 album with my mother's and Ron's faces on it, the cover I'd only ever stared at behind glass. My mother was twenty-six when she recorded it, the same age I am that afternoon.

My boyfriend, a French-horn player and pianist and singer who has performed at Carnegie Hall, has told me that of all the instruments he learned, the voice was the hardest. You can tell who someone is, he said. Your voice attests to who you are as a person.

Dee places the record on a turntable and lowers the needle, and just like that, minor-key guitar chords fill the air, and drumming, too, and then there's Ron, his real, albeit wobbly, slightly off-key and tinny voice, but his voice all the same, and from behind it there is a burst of full-bodied belting, to which Dee says, Your mother always had such a beautiful voice, and I close my eyes to listen harder because it is a voice I do not know, a voice I've never heard before: rich, robust.

Each note from the record player is a portal I want to pass through.

Dee wants to reminisce. Your mother had a real stage presence, she says. Jimi, meanwhile, was awful. Unbearably loud. He made my earrings vibrate, she says. She and Lloyd walked out in the middle of his set.

Before I leave—Dee and I will hang out a handful of times during my next two years in Tucson—she copies the vinyl onto a CD for me, even prints a small, square image of the album cover for its plastic case.

At home, I cannot stop listening, even though doing so feels like a betrayal. These are the forbidden tracks, the secret harmonies, the ones she did not want me to hear.

A throaty and upbeat alto:

> *Give me your laughter.*
> *Send it my way.*
> *Gather your children*
> *from the end of the day.*

I don't mind the trite lyrics. My mother is chanting "children." It feels prescient. Personal. *I'm right here!* I want to shout at her through the stereo.

I call my boyfriend, make him tolerate one insipid chorus after another. He's spent time with my mom. Like me, he cannot believe the voice is hers. His ears are professionally trained. I hold up the phone.

Listen, I demand. What do you hear?

What I hear, then and now: Virtuosity. Fervor. The kind of singing that requires the whole body and all of its breath. I imagine my mother belting with her chest out and arms wide, rolling her shoulders across octaves, standing on her toes.

I hear Janis Joplin telling Dick Cavett that singing is "letting yourself feel all those things that you have already on the inside of you but you're all the time trying to push them aside because they don't make for polite conversation."[17]

"That's the one reason I can sing," Janis told him. "Because I can just close my eyes and let all those things just come out."

I hear Jimi insisting that "music doesn't lie."

I even hear a man from an *America's Got Talent* clip I saw on a cross-country flight. The contestant wants the judges to know that he's there, onstage, for his family. He has six young kids, he says, and wants to show them "that if their dad can live out his dreams, then nothing's impossible for them." I am sandwiched between strangers in coach but cannot stop the tears, especially as the man's voice moves from timid to urgent. That's why I'd wanted to hear Mom's music all those years ago, I think. I wanted her to show me how art opens the artist, that exposure is a worthy endeavor.

*   *   *

I feel close to Mom during these listening sessions, as I admire the range and timbre of her voice, as I delight in her talent. Still, it is hard to say to whom I feel close: the woman I know, or the woman she used to be.

A memory. Mom has a surprise. I am six and gathered with my siblings in the living room.

No peeking, she calls.

We squeal. What could it be? A present? A visitor?

Ready or not! she says. A woman steps into view. Like it? she says.

It is my mother's voice. But it emerges from inside a wavy, shoulder-length bob. The mother I know has waist-long, pin-straight hair. I approach, tug on her locks until she protests.

It's not a wig, she says, shaking free. I got it cut. I got it permed.

Betrayal floods my veins. Who is this woman and where has my mother gone?

After leaving Ron, in 1971, Mom got a job as a record company assistant and strategized ways to slip her work into the stack of demos. Months in, she watched an executive scrape a pile of tapes into the trash. She was aghast.

Those are people with hopes! she said.

Said he, Rock stars come and go.

Just before she quit—the job, the industry, the dream—he asked her to forge autographs on portrait photos of famous rock stars. No one will know, he said. It keeps the people happy.

Ron produced over a dozen albums on little-known labels after their split, most of them folk-rock-esque. In 2014, he released a song whose chorus describes sitting atop a stoop in 1966 with his beautiful girlfriend. The lyrics don't say that she was a songwriter, too, that he permitted her a single solo on their twelve-track album even though her voice was far superior. They don't say that he made her play backup so often that eventually she backed right offstage.

In Fiction Workshop, I place my writing on the table, a literary offering, and steel myself against the onslaught. Classmates cite dead metaphors. Call my beloved protagonist a brat. One professor sketches a diagram for plot on the board when it's clear my story lacks one. They seem to agree on only one thing: I have a strong voice.

Sony Music Entertainment (Japan) rereleased Mom and Ron's 1971 album in 2001. And you can now buy her still-sealed first-press LP on eBay for three hundred dollars. You can also enjoy a few of her tracks on YouTube. I hadn't heard them in a while, so I clicked, discovered an eerie prophesy in her only solo, called "Take a Stand," about a couple's dissolution.

> *Don't speak of fate.*
> *And to say I should wait.*
> *It's too late.*
> *I can only think of what might have been.*

Janis Joplin once said that singing is "like loving somebody." I'm not sure that listening to singing is like receiving love, but hearing Mom croon fills me with tenderness—for her, for the magnitude of her forfeiture. I am a mother now, a writer. I want to be together in this creative space.

I dial her number. Can I play you something? I say.

I'm in a coffee shop, she says, but sure, go ahead.

I cue up her solo, hold the phone to the computer speaker. When I get back on the line, she is laughing in a surprised and semi-bashful way, like a chorus of waiters has just serenaded her with cake. Where did you get that? she asks with signature suspicion. Why are you listening to that?

Your voice, I say, is amazing. I use the present tense; surely the voice is still in her. Isn't it? In my teens and twenties it was easier to imagine her sloughing off this rock star persona like a skin she'd outgrown, emerging with cropped hair and small kids, leaving the old rind to wither in the sun. But I'm older now, and while my shape-shifts have been less extreme, I no longer think our layers expire. I think they just get reabsorbed. Rearranged. I believe, too, in Jimi's burning guitar: sometimes you sacrifice the things you love.

Mom thanks me, still claims she's subpar. The song is playing now, the music in both of our ears. The artistry's irrefutable.

She pivots, talks over it, asks if I'm reading anything interesting. I've just finished reading an article on the cosmos, on the myth that there's no sound in outer space. I tell her that 250 million light years away, a black hole is humming in a B-flat, fifty-seven octaves below middle C. Intergalactic music, I say, that no one will ever hear.

She reminds me that lots of animals make noises we can't distinguish. Like elephants. And bats.

Also, I think, humans.

DAUGHTER OF THE COMMANDMENTS

THE EMCEE HAS A gray ponytail and a bow tie and wants to meet some of the "phenomenal wild, weird, wacky, and wonderful kids who Courtney has invited to her bat mitzvah party!"

He approaches a table of seventh graders eating pigs in a blanket on a covered patio, sweating in the noonday sun. He pokes the mic under Nick's chin, says, Tell us about yourself. Nick pretends not to understand what the apparatus is and sniffs it, licks it. Nick is not a phenomenal, wild, weird, wacky, or wonderful friend. He's not even a friend. He's more like an asshole. His older brother is a star football player at the local high school, and this imbues Nick with by-proxy coolness that he maintains with attitude.

I have invited Nick for the same reason I have invited Anthony and Kyle and Francesca. The party is a chance for me to curate my social profile. Which is to say, improve it.

An hour earlier, at a nearby synagogue, I stood on the bema and chanted my haftarah from the Old Testament. I'd practiced this performance all year by listening to a cassette tape of the cantor, stopping and rewinding over each guttural inflection and operatic high note, following along in a color-coded book. I could decipher and pronounce the Hebrew—I'd attended Sunday school since first grade—but didn't understand the words. Like nearly all the Reform Jews I knew who partook in this rite of passage, I hadn't studied Hebrew as a language.

Afterward, I delivered the requisite speech, in English, explaining the Biblical excerpt in sentences spoon-fed to me by the rabbi. When Samuel retired from the court, I said, he wanted to know that he'd been a virtuous and fair judge, wanted a clear conscience. "Whose ox and donkey have I taken?" he asked his people—and I asked mine. "Whom have I betrayed?"

What was I even saying?

Lacy and Francesca had scuttled in late; I spotted them as I was thanking my family. Diana and Maggie whispered in the pews. Nick pretended to sleep with his mouth ajar. None of these kids were even Jewish; only a handful of my public school classmates were. They didn't understand history and tradition. My friends from sleepaway camp did, but they lived elsewhere—New Jersey and Long Island—and couldn't attend.

At least Wes seemed attentive. I had sought and spotted his blond head before the service even began.

*　*　*

That's us, me and Wes, months earlier in Home Ec. We're seated at the same table.

My fucking back, Wes said to no one in particular, twisting his torso left and right. He was stocky and thick, a football player, but with melancholic eyes and plump lips. He played the violin. We were learning to sew small animal pillows and we had both chosen to make whales, proof of our shared worldview. I need a hard surface, he said, grimacing. He put down the gray felt and cotton stuffing, slipped off his stool, and laid belly-down on the tile floor behind me. The two of us had hardly spoken—we'd attended different elementary schools, were new to each other in seventh grade—but I spied an opening.

Maybe you need a heating pad, I said over my shoulder. This is what I'd seen my father do. Or, you know, drugs. I felt twitchy and shrugged, bounced.

I need pressure, he said. Can you walk on it?

What?

I mean, not with your shoes on.

Mrs. S was across the room helping classmates make sheep. I blew aside my bangs and kicked off my bucks.

Wes's blue-jeaned butt was a perfect hump, the orange 8 of his jersey a ready-made trail. I advanced, toed his side. You sure? He laid his forehead on his knuckles, waited for me to mount.

I'd never stood on a human back. I placed a foot perpendicular to his frame and a hand on a nearby wall and pushed up. Wes grunted a little puff, then turned his face and smiled. His back skin slid and shifted beneath his shirt and I wobbled, steadied myself, giggled, said, Isn't this hurting you? I took tiny, unstable steps, held out my arms for balance. I could feel his muscles and tissues and ribs through my socks, could feel his shoulder blades and every knob of spine. A private topography. Warmth radiated up my legs. I wondered if he knew whale hearts are the size of cars.

The post–bat mitzvah party is at my grandparents' country club in Westchester County, New York, which they joined after being rejected by the anti-Semitic one up the street. It is June 1991, two weeks before my thirteenth birthday. On a daylit covered patio, a five-piece band jams "Hot Hot Hot" and adults form a conga line. *Ee-yes, girls!* Middle-schoolers drift toward a side table where the emcee has laid out loot: an AM-FM radio, headphones, a CD organizer. A Doors album. Once upon a time, my mother was in a band that opened for the Doors, but I don't think about this now, not even as she congas past in a skirt suit. *People in the party, hot hot hot!* I'm busy chatting up Wes, whom I've placed at my table. Assigned seats.

Admit you like this song, I say.

My favorite, he says. He lifts the small gumball machine by his place setting, turns it over in his hands, replaces it. This is the take-home gift I've selected for my friends. Several of them will consume all the gum that afternoon, competing to see who can create the biggest jaw-breaking wad. Wes rolls up his sleeves, reveals thick, tanned forearms. I wonder if this is the first bat mitzvah he's ever attended. I wonder if he knows that in the eyes of Jewish law, I am now a woman.

What I don't see, until I watch the VHS tape: Dad telling a group of fellow elementary school teachers, You know how I celebrated my bar mitzvah? In nineteen fifty-seven? Sponge cake and Manischewitz in the basement. Chuckles. None of this brass band shit.

My father is uneasy around money, not only because his parents, who died when I was small, had little, but because despite working tirelessly as an educator, he can't afford a party like this. My maternal grandpa, a prominent CEO, is footing the bill, just as he has for Jewish summer camp, just as he did for our family trip to Israel. Grandpa, who changed his surname to sound less Semitic a few decades prior, is invested in sowing our Jewish roots. All of us, maybe Dad most of all, are humbled by this generosity. Two years after Grandpa dies, I will marry the grandson of Baptist ministers, a union my grandfather would have protested—would likely even have rejected. I will visit his headstone and apologize.

A barely perceptible breeze blows in off Long Island Sound, wobbles the pastel balloon arches over our heads. Beyond a sweep of fresh-mowed grass, yachts glide by. *I'm hot, you're hot, he's hot!* I tug my white dress, smooth its tiered eyelet skirt. I'm warm, but don't dare remove my matching cropped jacket, the one whose shoulder pads minimize my head; I have stuffed my bra with cotton balls and worry that my chest looks lumpy. My purse contains more cotton in case I want to adjust. Reshape. In a few weeks, I'll upgrade to a sturdier material and Lacy will corner me in the school bathroom, insist that you can't go from an AAA-cup to a D-cup overnight. I can tell those are not your boobs, she will say. I will appreciate her concern, will remove the wads of paper towels I'd meticulously molded into flesh.

Wes turns to talk to Nick, and I approach Lacy and Francesca, all silk tank tops and miniskirts and everlasting legs. They flip their hair, appear faintly bored. *He's hot, she's hot!* Lacy had been my BFF in fifth and sixth grades—we memorized every song on the *Beaches* soundtrack, had back-to-back sleepovers, even split a heart necklace—but she's moved on to blonder confidants like Francesca and stopped returning my calls. Today, though, as she's embraced by my parents and siblings, she's behaving, again, like a friend.

What I don't see when I watch the video: The videographer going from table to table to record guests' messages. Tremendous job, they say, and, Mazel tov, and, We look forward to more of your exploits. I don't see the husband of a relative confusing me for my fifteen-year-old sister. Rachel, he says, dabbing his forehead with a napkin, you're a very, very special young woman. I don't see my tiny, aged great aunt Bea pull off thick black shades and say, in a cigarette-singed voice, Hello, darling, and, Happy bat mitzvah, and, Everything is absolutely gorgeous and done to perfection. She is alone at her table. In a few years, she will die alone, too, and won't be discovered for days, and we will all wonder what more we could've done.

When I receive the video in the mail, months after my bat mitzvah, I will not watch it for these kind missives. I will not watch it to relive the biggest birthday party of my life. I will watch it for clues. Indicators. Will study bodies flitting by in the background. This day will not turn out how I had hoped.

The band breaks into "Twist and Shout" and Maggie, Lacy, and I storm the floor, yell-sing into the mic—*Shake it, shake it, shake it, baby, now!*—wiggle down to the ground, all Ferris Bueller on a parade float. The emcee gestures to Francesca on the fringes, but she flicks her wrist at him. He sneers back, hand on hip. She will sneer at me like this all through high school. Nonetheless, junior year, on a vacation with a mutual friend, I will see her shoplift and will do the same, and because I will be less slick about it, we will all get caught.

What I don't see: Grandpa, silver hair combed back, arm around a septuagenarian in a loud purple dress. Marge. Marge's husband was Grandpa's colleague. Her son was my father's student. For years I thought Marge was clairvoyant.

This lady introduced Courtney's parents, Grandpa says to the camera. It might be the best job she ever did.

My parents will spend the next decade falling out of love. Their divorce will cut us all.

What are the middle names of our current president? the emcee asks. We are seated on the covered patio floor, vying for prizes. I'm behind Maggie, chewing my cuticles, checking my stockings for runs.

Hands shoot up. Correct, the emcee says. Herbert and Walker.

What part of the body is the coccyx?

Nick thrusts his groin forward, says, I'll show you a coccyx. Big laughs.

I've kissed only one boy—at sleepaway camp, the previous summer. We became a couple during archery when he announced he'd dated all the girls on the long wooden bench except for me. That Friday night, on a grassy hill, while campers danced on the basketball courts down below and Israeli music pumped from outdoor speakers, I yielded to his pleas to let him kiss me "for real." I marveled at the sliminess of his tongue circling mine, watched a cord of saliva follow him as he pulled away. Said he, Now, was that so bad?

I know a few girls in middle school who have had sex. I wonder if Wes has had sex.

Now, says the emcee, let's change things up. The organist teases out the opening of "True Blue" and a woman with large frosted hair channels Madonna. To be eligible for today's grand prize, says the emcee, each of you must choose a grown-up and invite them to dance. That's right, one of these fine-looking adults is secretly worth a Discman.

I grab my dad. Lacy picks my grandpa and guffaws as he jives and spins her. Wes picks Evelyn, the white-haired wife of Grandpa's college roommate. Evelyn's grandson will introduce me to my future husband a decade from now. *True love, you're the one I'm dreaming of!* She will also be the mystery winner. When the emcee makes the announcement, Evelyn will grin and Wes will raise his fists like a boxing champ and I will whistle and whoop.

What I don't see: Diana blowing an enormous bubble into the camera until it pops.

I grab my purse, hustle across the patio and into the clubhouse. The song "Havah Nagila" is about to begin and the accompanying dance involves bouncing and spinning and I don't want the cotton balls from my bra to tumble onto the floor. I pass the enlarged photo on my sign-in board, me as a toddler, arms outstretched. Always chasing a hug. I'm about to pass the bar, which is closed, when I see Nick sitting on a counter stool, plucking maraschino cherries from the garnish bin. Anthony and Kyle flank him. He is small and will stay small and when I hit a growth spurt sophomore year, he will lean across the aisle between the desks in Spanish class and call me Jolly Green Giant.

Nice of you to invite Joe, he shouts. He chews open-mouthed. What? I say. Who?

Joe Napolitano, he says, gums stained clown-red. Duh.

I don't know Joe Napolitano. Nor did I know he was part of their crew.

It's real messed-up, Nick says. You hurt his feelings. His friends sneer.

I roll my eyes, watch him snap up another cherry from the bin. I think, Maraschino cherries cause cancer. This is what my mother says. I think, My family is paying for each of those goddamn cherries. He spits out a stem.

If you're so upset by this, I say, you can leave.

Nick gasps, puts a hand up to his chest. You kicking me out? he says, voice raspy. You kicking me out of your Jewish party?

I hear the opening notes of "Havah Nagila" and dash past him to the ladies' room to unload my bra.

The photographer demands smiles. Courtney, you're making the weirdest faces, he says.

The wind is pushing my bangs in the wrong direction, I say. I'm trying to blow them into place. We are on the lawn beside the clubhouse, under a tree to avoid the sun.

I am posing with my mom and she has advice. Open your mouth a little, she says. Put your tongue on its roof, like this. When she was a singer, she also dabbled in modeling; the framed black-and-white headshots hang in our den. Lift your chin, she says. Wind blows in off the Long Island Sound, tousles us both.

You guys are like an ad for hair stuff, says the photographer.

I think, Why is Nick such a dick?

Says the photographer, Say "yesss"!

I think, Why didn't I invite Joe Napolitano?

Says the photographer, Say "moneyyy"!

What I don't see, and the videographer doesn't, either: Wes and Diana climbing the carpeted clubhouse steps to an off-limits upper floor. I don't see them scurry down a hallway or lean against the wall. I don't see Wes grab her waist—or does she grab his?—don't see their lips touch and their groins kiss.

I'm still not smiling right.

Mom tries a new tack: Courtney, say your boyfriend's name!

When we return from the photo session, the band is playing "From a Distance," and Grandpa, high on celebration, pulls my mother in for a slow dance, one of the few times in my life I'll see him show her affection. She winks at me before twirling away, and I feel a too-hard grip on my arm and my sister is there, her face in mine. I know the intensity of her expression—eyebrows screwed up, mouth tight.

Lacy and I were walking to the bathroom, she says, black blazer swallowing her slender frame. We saw them running upstairs. The patio darkens. Total eclipse. We followed, she says, and thank God. As in, *Imagine what they would have done if we hadn't.* As in, *They would've gone all the way at your bat mitzvah.*

My mother is speak-singing into the space by my grandfather's ear. *From a distance, there is harmony!*

Are you sure? I say, sour sting in my throat. Are you positive?

A salt-and-pepper couple taps me on the shoulder to say they have to leave early but they're proud of me and I'm so great, and I've never seen them before and I'm not so great, I'm the opposite of so great, and my sister squeezes my hand in commiseration and I can't squeeze back because I'm directing every ounce of energy into a simulated smile.

I will find Diana, ask if we can talk. We will sit near the girls' bathroom on a floral couch that clashes with her floral dress. I will not think about Samuel's speech on integrity and loyalty from my haftarah. Nor will I realize that Diana's father is a line cook at this club and likely helped prepare the lunch that's currently stuck in my teeth. Instead, I will flare my nostrils—my technique for stemming a cry—because I don't want anyone, least of all my family, asking me what's wrong.

But we only kissed twice, Diana will say. Not even twice.

The emcee beckons, Courtney, come on down! Dessert time. I will say nothing more to Diana this afternoon, and nothing about this ever to Wes. I am not his girlfriend. Never was. Never will be.

* * *

The videographer has arrived at my table. Maggie grabs the mic, runs a hand through her bangs. Maggie's real name isn't Maggie; her parents picked the moniker out of the phone book when they immigrated from India a decade before. In the coming months, Maggie will replace Lacy as my BFF. She and I will spend weekends at her parents' deli on North Avenue, and she will teach me how to use the cash register, which will zip and ding like a toy, and I will never appreciate the depth of her parents' financial stress. She will eat Shabbat dinners with my family and learn some Hebrew songs, and my father will place his hands on her head and pray for health and happiness. After dinner we will sprint upstairs and squeeze into my closet and guzzle wine coolers in the dark.

Hey, Courtney, Maggie says to the camera. I know you're a little upset today, no mentioning what it is, ahem. She reaches off-screen and the videographer follows and there's me seated, back turned, fiddling with a candy wrapper. My white shoulder pads are up to my ears.

Maggie tells me I look beautiful. She says she hopes I feel better. She leans over and kisses my cheek. I don't reciprocate. I don't turn around.

Before he leaves, Nick will scribble Joe Napolitano's name on my sign-in board in purple permanent marker, a board that still hangs in my childhood bedroom. Joe will wind up being one of just a few fellow athletes in my academic track, and we will become friendly, will call each other by our respective last names. I will envy how unstressed he always seems, how he doesn't need to study, even in BC calculus, the hardest math class offered at our school. On Saint Patrick's Day senior year, already admitted to college, we will both be part of a crew that skips school and hops a Metro-North train to Manhattan and drinks from bottles in paper bags. We will all get lost at the parade.

These people, whose blinks created hurricanes: I will lose track of them. I will hear bits and pieces from hometown hangers-on, see snapshots on social media, will learn that Nick became a banker and Diana, a health-care worker. That Wes got divorced and remarried.

In December 2012, Joe Napolitano will OD on heroin. The funeral parlor will set up a memorial website, and when I post a condolence note, I will see the names of several kids from my bat mitzvah party, a perverse virtual reunion. I will think about how these notes regret not Joe's onetime absence, but his eternal one. I will click through photos—Joe as a toddler gumming a pipe, teenage Joe embracing his grandpa—and will feel confused by the intensity of feelings that well up inside me for this boy-turned-man I hardly knew. More recent snaps will reveal the gauntness of his face, eyes ringed in gray, a disconnected stare. When I see the digital candle with a message, MISS YOU, LOVE MAMA, I will burst into tears. I have just become a mother.

How much we cared, I will think, about our own reflections.

Note from Diana in my seventh-grade yearbook: "I'm really sorry about what happened at your bat mitzvah."

TRESPASS

I AM FOUR MONTHS a mother, a fact proclaimed by my son's age. We will be forever tethered to each other by time, two hands on a clock. I don't think much about this until after his birth.

I am four months a mother and have returned to work and need to pump every few hours. This is not only to have milk that the babysitter can bottle-feed to Oliver, not only to relieve pain in my chest or avoid clogged ducts and infection. I need to pump because without a baby constantly at my breast, my supply will dry up and I won't be able to feed my son at all. My blind body accepts that the robotic suction is a hungry baby's mouth.

I am four months a mother when I call my mother for help. I work as a college application essay specialist in the suburban county where I grew up, an hour away from where I live with my husband and son. It is the community in which my father teaches, though he now lives with a new partner in Manhattan. It is the community in which my divorced, single mother still resides.

I have called my mother because I can't figure out how to be a professional while breastfeeding. Where to pump? I tell her I had an academic job interview in New Jersey two weeks before and didn't feel comfortable asking my would-be boss if there was a place to relieve full breasts and so wound up in the bathroom of a pizzeria by the train station. Pumping sessions take at least twenty minutes, and I tell her how the customers knocked and then banged on the door and that I emerged into a cluster of disapproving eye-rolls and head wags. Last week, I say, I pumped in my parked car, but it turns out that disrobing in daylight and affixing plastic shields and tubes to your breasts while your nipples are visibly tugged and squeezed unnerves passersby.

I have four clients on Tuesday afternoon, I say, and each session is an hour long, and my body will need relief. I have nowhere to go.

I am four months a mother and my tutorial workspaces are dining tables lit by chandeliers and kitchen tables strewn with bills. All of my bosses are mothers. They are the ones who hire me, the ones who pay me, the ones who worry over the phone about their children's futures.

My roster of students includes a teenager whose father died in a terrorist attack. He doesn't remember much—he was little—but is regularly told how much he looks and sounds and acts like his father. I gnaw the fleshy inside of my cheek as he describes what it feels like to wear his father's face. How agonizing it must be for his mother, I think, to watch her son grow into her late husband. Or maybe, I think, how beautiful. I am four months a mother and want to hug the woman in the other room, widowed in the most heinous and violent way, sole parent to a child who will depend on her for everything, and I feel the pressure in my chest—all grief and fluid and fear—when I tell her, insufficiently, that I am sorry.

I ask Mom, Can I come by after my second tutoring? To pump?

She is quiet, says, To my house?

Her house was once our house. It is the house in which I grew up, from the age of two until I left for college. I am four months a mother and still unused to that pronoun: *my*. I suck on it like an ice cube. It anesthetizes my tongue.

The second-floor bedroom with the fuzzy blue carpet bears all my marks. Faint dots on the walls from Fun-Tak that held up posters of my paramours: Bon Jovi and Eddie Vedder. A wooden desk in whose drawer I scratched my initials with a Swiss Army knife. The twin bed I hid beneath when home alone, petrified of any ghostly noise I discerned. Beside it is the radio to which I pressed my head long after I should've been asleep to hear *Love Phones* on Z100, so eager to find out what men wanted. That's the mattress on which I applied what I learned.

In the closet: stiff *Archie* comics and letters from sleepaway camp and ballet slippers that belonged to a beloved friend who died in fifth grade and the mustard-colored safe I received for Hanukkah and into which I stuffed Zima and clove cigarettes. Also, a swirly painting of a fetus in utero I made for Mom one Mother's Day in junior high and snatched back in high school when I found it in the attic. I had wanted her to hang it up. I was always so full of wanting.

Yes, I tell my mother. I want to come to your house. She has kept my room more or less intact. With four other bedrooms, she doesn't need the space.

I have an appointment, she says. I won't be here. The implication: if she's not there, I can't be either.

It's not personal, she says when I protest, which I do repeatedly.

She had the locks changed after Dad moved out, seven years prior, and won't give keys to anyone—not her children or the neighbors or the cleaning lady. Nor will she order anything off the internet or leave her dog tied up outside a store or record her own voice on the answering machine. Fear is an omnivore.

Her decision is not personal, but I feel it in my person. In the seize of my stomach. In the cramp in my jaw. In the gash that appears when I tear my thumb with my teeth.

I say, Don't you trust me?

Yes, she says, but this is what makes me comfortable. Her words are another locked door. There's no way through, no explanation beyond. Five years earlier, during a difficult stretch in our relationship, one of her friends had taken me aside, asked,

Can your mother do anything to show that she trusts you, besides giving you a house key?

I'd answered too readily: No.

I am four months a mother and my mother is four months a grandmother and she visits us often in Brooklyn. She will become the grandma who laughs the loudest, who attends birthday parties and piano recitals, whose pocketbook produces gag gifts, as it did in my youth—whoopee cushions and Groucho Marx glasses and gummy eyeballs. She is the woman who made me into an artist, the one who will encourage my children's creativity too. Still, she didn't breastfeed, and can't appreciate why I'm so committed. What's the big deal about formula? she says often. Plenty of mothers use formula and their kids are fine.

I am four months a mother and it is winter in New York and everything is a shade of shadow: the sky, the trees, the street. At a long, narrow dining table, I work with a student on an essay about adventuring, while a dog sleeps at my feet. This sixteen-year-old hiked Mount Rainier to watch the sunrise, went scuba diving in Belize, chased fresh powder on the steepest slopes. I like to take risks, he tells me, to feel adrenaline in my veins. How undaunted he seems. How intrepid. As we say goodbye, I wonder if this makes his mother nervous.

I set out toward my childhood home, and am quickly unsettled by how lonesome it seems. The mammoth maple I used to climb, centerpiece of our front yard, contracted a disease and croaked. The grass is patchy and frosted. A shingle has slipped off the roof. I zip into the driveway, the same driveway my grandpa, my mother's father, would glide into in his Cadillac on Sundays, unannounced. If my father answered the door and we kids weren't home, my grandpa would leave without saying hello to my mother. I'd hear about this afterward. Sometimes I'd find her crying. My whole childhood, I watched her crave her parents' attention and affection. I never saw them kiss her, never heard them say *I love you*. How does one learn to give if one has not received?

After a few days of pleading—Let me think about it, she said on Sunday; I'm figuring out how this would work, she said on Monday—my mother has agreed to leave a key, so long as I return it to its hiding place before I go. I shut off the car and decide this is a meaningful gesture. Maybe, since I'm four months a mother and she's four months a grandmother, it signifies a shift. Maybe she will get increasingly comfortable leaving the key and eventually offer me one to keep.

I will be wrong about this. She won't leave the key again. In fact, on a future visit, when Oliver is three and I have a new infant, we will arrive earlier than planned and Mom won't be home yet and Oliver will have to poop and he will do so in the woods beside the house—her house. Mom, when she finally arrives, will try to downplay it, will say, It's like camp!, but what will pass over her face for just a second, a cloud eclipsing the sun, will be sadness. Guilt. Mom cannot help this web of distrust, never meant for it to ensnare us all.

Today, though, when I am four months a mother, I have access for the first and last time. I follow her instructions: step behind a bush near the side door, locate the green watering can and the slate tile beneath it and the plastic bag beneath that, inside of which is the key. Bingo! I rub the metal between my fingers. It is thicker than any others I've seen. Heavier too. More difficult to duplicate.

My breasts hurt. I slide the key into the lock and the teeth bite and I push open the door into one of the most familiar physical spaces I know, all blond wood and whimsical tchotchkes, and also the most familiar sound: a beeping alarm. Blood glugs in my gut. This wasn't supposed to happen. At the keypad, I punch in the numbers I remember from childhood, but they don't register—of course they don't register—because not only has my mother changed the locks; she has changed the code. I try her birthday, try all 1s, something easy because Mom has a fragile memory, try numbers in a row and numbers in a square, and the buttons squish under my sweaty fingers, and the system now assumes that I'm an unwelcome visitor, a thief, a criminal, and all at once the volume swells and a siren wails and a mechanized voice explodes through the wall: *You have violated a protected area! The police were called! Leave immediately!*

I fumble for my phone, call my mother, plug the other ear. No answer.

A lactating body is sensitive to sound. It assumes loud noise is a wailing, hungry baby, and responds in kind: my breasts bulge and harden and cramp.

It is 3:15. I have to be at the next student's house at 3:45. The only way my milk will let down is if I'm relaxed. I am not relaxed. Prickles of panic climb my arms. I cannot take a deep breath. Amid the earsplitting distress signal and robotic commands—*Leave! Immediately!*—I withdraw the plastic funnels and valves and membranes and tubes from my bag and pull off my shirt and swap my nursing bra for a strapless bra designed to hold these parts in place. I fasten two small eight-ounce bottles, one on each side.

The phone on the wall rings, nearly inaudible inside the tumult. An alarm company employee. He needs to ensure I'm a resident and not an intruder. He asks for the secret password. I do not have the secret password. So many ways to be walled out.

I'm the daughter, I shout. Childhood home, I say, misunderstanding. My breasts deliver one fat drop apiece. I cannot bear to watch.

They will be dispatching someone to the property, he says. Protocol.

Six minutes until the police arrive. I know this from childhood. I sit at the kitchen table, in the same chair I occupied for our family meals. The table at which my father tutored after school and on weekends, all yellow legal pads and chewed Bic pen caps, a space as insignificant to his students as my students' kitchens are to me.

Taped to the wall to my right, a vertical poster that reads
EAT EAT EAT until the bottom prong of the final *E* disap-
pears as if into a mouth and *EAT* becomes *FAT*. A sign that
sapped pleasure out of every childhood bite and once caused an
overweight friend to burst into tears. A mantra that befit my
mother's restrictive diet and my grandmother's, too, that evoked
the one time I recall Grandma ever coming over for lunch, how
she removed from her purse a single hard-boiled egg, which
she placed in the center of her plate. This is all I need, she said.
Later, in adulthood, I will think, Even their lips were locked.

One ounce per bottle. Oliver eats six ounces per meal. I need
more time. More air. More mercy. I pull up baby pictures on
my phone, all huge eyes and cheeks and toothless gums. EAT
EAT LIVE.

The alarm's an electric current. *Violated!* It vibrates the hairs
on my arms, swings the papier-mâché parrot hanging from
the ceiling, threatens to dislodge the Post-its affixed to my
mother's fridge. *Protected!* See my family assembled around the
counter there? It's Friday night, Shabbat, and we've lit a ceramic
candelabra on whose base is a miniature Adam and Eve and a
demonic red snake. My mother is baking honeyed apples and
the air is sweet and warm and we're taking turns expressing
gratitude, saying nice things we did that week—I told Val
I liked her dress, I say—and my father puts his hands on my
mother's bowed head—Blessed are You, Lord our God, King
of the Universe—and my siblings and I poke our faces into the
tent their bodies make. Home.

One siren overwhelms the other. A cruiser has pulled up alongside my car in the driveway and red and blue lights swirl around the kitchen. I shut off the pump and disassemble the parts and quickly pull on my shirt.

Two officers are framed in the doorway, a sight that would have made me panic as a teenager, would've induced guilt even if I'd done nothing wrong. How many times I'd stumbled through this door drunk or high or in the aftermath of making out, convinced that my parents would smell me, would know.

Sorry, I shout. No emergency. I feel heat in my bra. I'm the homeowner's daughter, I say. My left breast, the more prolific one, has sprung a leak. A dark blossom unfurls on my shirt. I cross my arms. One of the men asks how to spell my name, writes it down. My mom was supposed to leave the house unarmed, I say. I don't say, *She was supposed to do this because she wasn't comfortable giving me the code.* I don't say, *It's not personal.*

My phone vibrates. Oh, shit, Mom says when she hears what's happening. Shit, shit. I hand her to a cop.

I will pack up my stuff in haste—already late for the next appointment—and won't properly affix the bottlecaps. On the drive home that night, I will simmer and fizz and yearn. When I arrive in Brooklyn, the base of my bag will be sticky and damp and the bottles will be empty.

CHAOS THEORY

I WANT TO TELL you about broken glass. About the blue orb wrapped in cloth that my husband crushed with his heel at our wedding ceremony, just before the kiss. I want to tell you about a Jewish tradition meant to invoke a demolished temple. Meant to remind us that joy should not override attention to the world's disrepair. Meant to remind us that a marriage lives always under the threat of a heel.

I want to tell you about symbolism, about retrieving the blue shards from the floor beneath the wedding canopy and placing them into a tiny glass tube alongside Hebrew prayers on parchment. A personalized mezuzah. According to Jewish law and lore, hanging that finger-sized mezuzah in one's doorjamb ensures long lives for all inhabitants and wards off evil. My husband and I placed the mezuzah on a shelf by our apartment door and meant to hang it up, but then our son was born and we were consumed and amid the consumption the mezuzah got knocked to floor and our wedding shards became wedding slivers.

I want to tell you about romance, about how my husband recovered what pieces he could from the jagged mess and glued them to a little board and put the little board in a little frame and gifted the whole thing to me for our anniversary. I want to tell you, too, that we meant to hang it by our apartment door, but then our second son was born and we were consumed and amid the consumption the frame with the broken mezuzah with the broken glass got knocked to floor and our wedding slivers became wedding specks.

I want to tell you about surrender. About how my husband and I decided not to frame the broken frame with the broken mezuzah with the broken glass.

Did we believe the universe was sending us a message? Did we know what the message was? Did we really think that in a galaxy with thirty billion planets, and on a planet with over seven billion people, energy from outer space traveled millions of light years to Earth and to the United States and to New York, that it slipped into the windows of our third-floor Brooklyn apartment and whispered in our ears and asked us to listen?

I want to tell you, *Yes*.

In the Manhattan office of Dr. S, someone who has saved me from anxiety's shape-shifting intrusions countless times over a dozen years, someone with whom I discuss how DNA informs experience and experience can alter DNA, I describe a circumstance as "written in the stars." I have just returned from a summer trip to Greece, where I am part of the faculty in a writing program. For weeks I listened to colleagues discuss ancient myths and knit them into poetry. I hiked to a seaside cave where sailors left offerings to the Dioscuri—twins immortalized in the constellation Gemini—for protection at sea. Each evening, I ambled home beneath an enormous, shimmering sky, pausing every few steps to tip back my head and marvel.

My psychiatrist cocks her head. If you want to talk stars, she says, you should call this astrologist. She lifts her iPad, scrolls for contact info, adds, She will blow your mind.

My mind is blown already. My go-to authority on neurobiology and psychopharmacology and evidence-based practices not only condones consigning one's fate to the zodiac, but recommends it?

But, I say, you're a scientist. As if she were unaware.

Dr. S nods and says, Science is crucial to understanding ourselves, she says. But it's not sufficient.

Summer 1993. Carnival Day at sleepaway camp. I was in the oldest unit and we were helping to run afternoon events. A natural dramatist, I signed up to play the fortune-teller. I wore a kerchief on my head and large hoop earrings and sat on a tie-dyed tarp inside a tent. When younger kids stopped in, I flipped their hands over, ran a knowing finger along their palms. I pointed to life lines and love lines and—my own addition—camp lines, which anticipated the tenor of their summers. I prophesized Banquet dates and Color War wins and soccer successes. I told one boy he would father eight children. Told a girl she would master a new skill. I spoke as if each trellis of fleshly grooves were encoded, as if I bore the gift of decryption.

They all knew I was a fellow camper, a charlatan, a fictionist. Still, I would swear that for a few blinks, I saw their eyebrows lift into the promise of my predictions. I felt the current of wonder under their skin. *What if?*

Maybe I was the susceptible one. A few years later, a college friend's offhand comment would cast an unshakable shadow. He was a business major, a practical person, good with assessment.

That's us, lounging on a restaurant patio close to the under-grad dorms.

You strike me as someone who has bad luck, he said between sips of beer. In memory, the comment hinged on nothing I'd said or done that suggested misfortune. My stomach sputtered. I was nineteen, permeable, my fingernails colored with paint. I wondered if he was reading the world in a way I didn't know how to.

I tried to bury this judgment but it kept resurfacing. When I was hospitalized the following year because of a reckless mis-diagnosis. When my apartment flooded and turned a box of handwritten journals into inky mush. As I ricocheted between acrimoniously divorcing parents, and when my laptop was stolen in Baltimore and my wallet in New York, the words bobbed to the surface. *You are a person who has bad luck.*

My life, like most lives of relative privilege, is not unlucky. It is an amalgam. It has love and pleasure and stress and sadness and hard work. I didn't believe my friend's judgment, not really, but I couldn't dismiss it either. A scrape that didn't hurt, but wouldn't heal. Maybe it's because, while I heed provable data, I also respect how much of existence we cannot explain.

The astrologist my doctor recommends is a critical theorist. She has been reading birth charts on the side for twenty-five years because she thinks they hold surprising accuracies and weird perceptions. Her modest Brooklyn apartment transmits Victorian vibes: dark woods and deep reds and gold-framed paintings. I place her in her sixties. She wears a headband.

I tell her I've never met with an astrologist. She explains the practice's origins, the Greeks and Egyptians who studied nighttime reflections in buckets of water, who observed patterns on high. Whenever Mars trafficked into the constellation of Scorpio, she told me, there were accidents at sea. That's how they came to associate extraterrestrial energies with earthly dynamics.

I nod, take out my notebook, write: "energies, accidents." I do not think: mezuzah.

I am here because I believe in my erudite psychiatrist, and she believes in this erudite astrologist.

Astrology, Dr. S has said, gives destiny a role. It gives us a way to exist on Earth that's judgement-free.

I don't admit this outright, even to myself, but I want to be converted.

Dr. S: It can be liberating—a relief—to realize we're not in control.

It is the kind of thing she might have said about my limited influence as a parent to two sons who move in their own orbits.

I want it all, liberation and relief. I want to trust that a bout of insoluble chest pain and shallow breaths isn't just because of insufficient sleep or disordered thinking or defective biochemistry but because of planetary behavior. I want less self-blame. More cosmic reassurance.

I have sent the astrologist my birth data via email. At her mahogany dining table, where we sit, she hands me a printout of a circle divided into twelve sections. Each pie piece is tagged with a zodiac sign and filled with tiny graphic planets. This, she says, is what the sky looked like the moment you were born.

Astrology interprets the energies of the sun and moon and celestial bodies as human needs, she says. It's like having ten children. You must attend to all of them.

That's me, nodding and taking notes so I don't miss a thing.

You have three planets in Cancer, she says. This roots me firmly in the traits associated with my sun sign—one about which I know practically nothing. Cancer, she says, is ruled by the crab, an animal that traffics between the sea and the shore and the sea and the shore and the sea and the shore. Her repetition emphasizes the tenacious zigzag. It also proves entrancing. For Cancer, she says, the project is bringing the stuff from the sea onto the shore, the stuff from the sea onto the shore, the stuff from the sea onto the shore. There is something about this language and imagery—of legs scuttling to and fro and lapping waves—that turns me into a child listening to a story. Still, I don't know what she means.

What shore? I ask. What sea?

The astrologist pauses, closes her eyes, holds still. An unusually long moment passes during which I try not to move; I don't want to break her concentration, her commitment to clarity, precision. Her lids and mouth open simultaneously. The imaginal realm, she says.

Imaginal? It's not a word I've heard.

She nods. The nature of Cancer is bringing stuff from the imaginal into the real.

Sometimes I imagine my funeral. In quiet moments or when I'm upset, unsolicited images may arise of peopled pews and a wooden casket and my husband addressing a crowd. Often I can hear him, as if from a distance—muffled flatteries, his voice cracked with grief. The scene has changed through the years. Aged. Now my small sons sit in the front row, kicking their legs with impatience and incertitude, unaware of how this loss may reverberate.

In the aftermath of these visions, I hug and kiss everyone in my lived life with extra fervor. As if to apologize. As if to supply comfort for a time of would-be need. I wonder about the role of such a fantasy and why it recurs, especially since it frightens me to consider causing pain to those I love most. Perhaps it's a warning to invest in my health. A subconscious push to be a better partner or mother so that I'll be remembered as such. Or maybe it's a perverse way of managing anxiety. As if by naming a worst-case scenario, by immersing in it, I can reach around and measure its dimensions. I can be relieved, in some tiny way, of uncertainty and the discomfort it kindles.

I want to tell the astrologist that my life's work is translating amorphous, indeterminate imaginings into concrete prose, that I invent whole worlds into existence. But she has moved on.

There's something that can be challenging in your chart. She points to Mars, situated in a pie piece marked VIRGO. Mars has an antenna for problems and difficulties, she says. When Mars is attached to Virgo, it creates fear.

I watch her finger the red line connecting Mars to Neptune, god of the Sea. She wants to know if I've seen *Cast Away*, the survival drama in which a man's plane crashes in the South Pacific and leaves him stranded on an island.

I don't tell her I've seen the film several times, even though I'm not fond of most Hollywood fare. Nor do I describe the scene that makes me sob most. It unfolds when the character played by Tom Hanks is improbably rescued after years of starvation and solitude. Back home, he learns there was a funeral for him and discovers that his beloved, played by Helen Hunt, has married someone else. They've had a kid. Helen's character is beside herself: stunned, crushed, guilt-ridden.

Can you imagine? I say to my husband, through tears and snot, when we watch the movie together. I can't tell whom I'm crying harder for, Tom or Helen. Probably their mutual devastation.

Maybe it evokes the beach trip my husband and I took when I was six months pregnant with our firstborn, how he decided to go for a quick jog along the shore—twenty minutes, tops, he said—how after thirty minutes he hadn't returned and I lifted the back of my lounger, put on my glasses, how after forty minutes I stood and squinted down the beach, how I saw only laughing strangers, how I rubbed my belly and refused to entertain thoughts of an accident or a disappearance or to forecast what it would be like to have this baby alone, how after forty-five minutes I willed every distant shape to transfigure into his body and how one of them complied, and when he finally emerged, slightly sunburned and glassy with sweat—I found some cool shells, he said—I stumbled toward him in the sand, knees wobbling.

Can you imagine, I say to him during the movie, burying one life and commencing a new one, only to discover that your first love, maybe your true love, is still alive?

The astrologer's question has nothing to do with star-crossed lovers. Rather, she tells me, the positioning of the planets suggests a terror within me. When you have Neptune on the ascendant, she says, you have the capacity to imagine in any moment all the possibilities of that moment. It's like you're taking an accounting of everything to be frightened of.

I want to tell you that I became a convert in this moment. That my doubts about astrology receded like the tide. I want to say that every appraisal she made in this meeting resulted in my staring into the cavity of myself and nodding with vigor. I want to.

I want to tell you, too, about storytelling. How my drive to bring the imaginal into the real is accompanied by a fondness for narrative, for beginnings and endings. How I delight in transformation, not only in characters on the page, but as a writer, as a reader. How I can feel pulverized and remade by stories—a glass orb turned into a pile of shimmering shards turned into a framed work of art. How I seek this experience in real life too.

Part of the project of life, the astrologer says, is to live in concert with our vulnerabilities, even as we live with our gifts.

I want to tell you that all of her insights are this astute. That through her reading, I am rebuilt. Made anew.

She moves her finger around the page, says, There's an orderliness to how you think.

I am an associative, scattered thinker. I think the way I clean my apartment: while folding laundry I notice my son's inhaler on the shelf and walk to the kitchen to place it in the cabinet, whereupon I notice dishes in the sink and begin to scrub them.

I bite my lip.

You feel torn, she says, between your profession and your partnership, between work and family. You have to figure out how to navigate those conflicting needs.

I consider all the working partners and parents I know. I wonder for whom this isn't true.

She tells me that part of me is a homebody and another part of me is in the world.

I feel suddenly emboldened, say, Is that not the case for everyone?

Oh god, no, she says. For some people, feeling safe is about getting on a plane and going somewhere.

She must detect wariness; my face always gives me away.

Like I need beauty to feel nurtured, she adds. I would check out of an ugly hotel room if I had to stay there for any length of time. I just can't bear it. I feel unsafe.

I try to look as though I understand. I do not understand. She feels threatened by decor? She would squander the cost of a hotel room because of it?

* * *

I want to tell you about the placebo effect. How research shows that our belief in a treatment's benefits makes it more effective. How this phenomenon applies to prescription medication. Scientists have demonstrated these results over and over again.

Every time you ingest a pill, Dr. S has said, it's an act of faith. You are accepting the possibility that you can feel better.

I want you to know that the reverse applies too. That doubts about one's treatment will make it less effective.

The astrologist tells me I have a really lovely chart and a lot of gifts. As I ride the elevator to the ground floor, I imagine myself as a crab, sinking into the sea.

That night, I look up my sign. I learn that Cancers are linked to Artemis, daughter of Zeus, a huntress. Legend says that immediately after Artemis's own arrival, she helped with the birth of her twin brother, Apollo. Various astrologers consider Cancer the most maternal and nurturing of all the signs. I think of my beautiful sons. I think how I want to own this association, want to devour it, want to possess it. Also, I want to know whose company I keep. I google other people born on June 28. Fellow nurturers. I learn that a man born on this day in 1491 became king. I share a birthday with Henry VIII.

* * *

Lately, my son Oliver, age seven, has been trying to influence his lot.

During board games, just before he rolls the dice: I never get any points.

On our walk to the bookstore: They definitely won't have what I want.

Sometimes I fall for his setup. There's a huge kids' section, I say. I'm sure we'll find the book you're looking for.

No! He widens his eyes. Whenever I say that something won't happen, it does, he says. If I say it will happen, it doesn't.

Oh, right, I say. I bet the book's sold out.

I want to tell you a story, one you've probably heard before. It's about someone who loses the will to live, and dies. It's about someone else who insists on life, and lives.

I want to tell you about my maternal grandmother, paralyzed after a stroke, who wanted to call it quits. My number is up, she told me months into her suffering, but nobody will call it. It's about how her body persisted, emaciated and diapered, against her will, for ten long years.

I want to tell you that stories impose order onto chaos. Offer control over our lives and destinies. And isn't control a kind of salvation? This, I think, is what we seek in astrology and therapy and mezuzahs on doorposts. All of us just want to be saved.

Maybe the key is devotion. Maybe the route to relief is in whatever you believe.

I tell Dr. S about my session with her astrologist. Some details seemed apt, I say. Others, not so much.

Says she: I believe more in the concept of astrology than the practice of it.

I am perplexed. Wasn't the astrologist her suggestion? Also, though, I know what she means.

Dr. S asks my sign, nods when I tell her, as if the information makes sense. As if she does believe in the practice, despite her claim. As if she believes and disbelieves at once.

Cancers are healers, she offers. The Dalai Lama is a Cancer.

I ask her what I have in common with the Dalai Lama.

You're a writer, she says, as if I were unaware. Practitioners of the aesthetic arts connect us to one another and offer a context for pain.

I want to tell you I believe her. I want to. I do.

NOTES

1. Chris Sommerfeldt and Stephen Rex Brown, "Sicko Gynecologist Who Sexually Abused Two Patients Avoids Jail Time," *New York Daily News*, published March 29, 2016. https://www.nydailynews.com.

2. Graham Kates, "Attorney: More women joining lawsuit against Columbia Univ., doctor accused of sex abuse," CBSNews.com, published December 14, 2018. https://www.cbsnews.com/news/attorney-more-women-will-join-lawsuit-against-columbia-university-doctor-accused-of-sex-abuse.

3. Richard Cohen, "Even by his standards, Trump's welcome of Viktor Orban is in a class of its own," *The Washington Post*, published May 20, 2019. https://www.washingtonpost.com/opinions/even-by-his-standards-trumps-welcome-of-viktor-orban-is-in-a-class-of-its-own/2019/05/20/97490ca8-7b3b-11e9-a5b3-34f3edf1351e_story.html.

4. Janell Ross, "Police officers convicted for fatal shootings are the exception, not the rule," NBCNews.com, published March 13, 2019. https://www.nbcnews.com/news/nbcblk/police-officers-convicted-fatal-shootings-are-exception-not-rule-n982741.

5. Mapping Police Violence, accessed September 3, 2020. https://mappingpoliceviolence.org.

6. Ibid.

7. The United States Department of Justice, "Attorney General William P. Barr Delivers Remarks at the Grand Lodge Fraternal Order of Police's 64th National Biennial Conference," published August 12, 2019. https://www.justice.gov/opa/speech/attorney-general-william-p-barr-delivers-remarks-grand-lodge-fraternal-order-polices-64th.

8. Kanya Bennett, "Trump Just Gave Thousands of Bayonets and Hundreds of Grenade Launchers Back to Police," ACLU.org, published August 28, 2017. https://www.aclu.org/blog/criminal-law-reform/reforming-police/trump-just-gave-thousands-bayonets-and-hundreds-grenade.

9. Conor Friedersdorf, "Police Have a Much Bigger Domestic-Abuse Problem Than the NFL Does," *The Atlantic*, published September 19, 2014. https://www.theatlantic.com/national/archive/2014/09/police-officers-who-hit-their-wives-or-girlfriends/380329.

10. Olivia B. Waxman, "How the U.S. Got Its Police Force," *Time*, published May 18, 2017. https://time.com/4779112/police-history-origins.

11. Chelsea Hansen, "Slave Patrols: An Early Form of American Policing," National Law Enforcement Museum Blog: On the Beat, published July 10, 2019. https://lawenforcementmuseum.org/2019/07/10/slave-patrols-an-early-form-of-american-policing/#_edn1.

12. Ben Fountain, "Slavery and the Origins of the American Police State," Medium, published September 13, 2018. https://gen.medium.com/slavery-and-the-origins-of-the-american-police-state-ec318f5ff05b.

13. German Lopez, "American police shoot and kill far more people than their peers in other countries," Vox, published November 14, 2018. https://www.vox.com/identities/2016/8/13/17938170/us-police-shootings-gun-violence-homicides.

14. "Gun Violence in America," Everytown for Gun Safety Support Fund, published May 19, 2020. https://everytownresearch.org/report/gun-violence-in-america.

15. Tom Jackman, "Fraternal Order of Police union endorses Trump, *The Washington Post*, published September 16, 2016. https://www.washingtonpost.com/news/true-crime/wp/2016/09/16/fraternal-order-of-police-union-endorses-trump.

16. United States, Office of the Press Secretary, "Remarks by President Trump to Law Enforcement Officials on MS-13," published July 28, 2017. https://www.whitehouse.gov/briefings-statements/remarks-president-trump-law-enforcement-officials-ms-13.

17. Steve Inskeep and Laura Sydell, "Janis Joplin: The Queen of Rock," National Public Radio, 50 Great Voices, Transcript, published June 7, 2010. https://www.npr.org/transcripts/127483124.

ACKNOWLEDGMENTS

Incalculable thanks to Rebecca Gradinger, for believing in this book from its infancy and fighting hard for it; Amanda Uhle, for saying Yes at every turn and expertly wearing all the hats; and Rita Bullwinkel, for editorial heroism and bigheartedness.

To the entire McSweeney's team: Your commitment to an outfit so full of integrity and humor is a boundless gift.

To Hannah Beresford, whose literary prowess is matched only by her kindness; and Andrea Chapin, for wisdom and generosity, bar none.

For sentences read, advice dispensed, and literary camaraderie: Tomás Q. Morín, Patrick Phillips, Mary Gaitskill, Maura Sheehy, Jennifer Cody Epstein, Alison Lowenstein, the much-missed Sarah Coleman, T Kira Madden, Cam Terwilliger, Cara Blue Adams, Tiphanie Yanique, Mitchell S. Jackson, Elisa Albert, Mat Johnson, Joshua Wolf Shenk, Chloe Weiss, Dan Mandel, Emily Nestler, Jessica Pavone, and Kelli Geller. Extra love to Julia Lichtblau for all the strengthened sentences, homemade meals, and political outrage. Caroline Bornstein: thanks for graciously letting me trail you around.

To the professors who put life-changing books into my hands and gave me direction when I most needed it: Aurelie Sheehan, Elizabeth Evans, Jason Brown, Alice McDermott, Jean McGarry, and the late Stephen Dixon.

I'm appreciative of the institutions and organizations whose support ensured I stayed the course, including Johns Hopkins University, the University of Arizona, the Center for Fiction, and the Brooklyn Writers Space. Extra love to MacDowell, in whose enchanting woods I composed seminal parts of this book.

Enormous thanks to the US editors and judges who first selected some of these pieces for publication or distinction: Emily Nemens, Nadja Spiegelman, Deborah Kim, Sonja Livingston, Shelly Oria, Hilton Als, and Rebecca Solnit.

To the Sunday Times Short Story Award judges whose votes of confidence, prize money, and advocacy continue to buoy my progress in countless ways: Tessa Hadley, Sebastian Faulks, Petinah Gappah, Mark Lawson, and the delightful Andrew Holgate.

I'm grateful to everyone at Fletcher & Company, particularly Veronica Goldstein, Elizabeth Resnick, and Sarah Fuentes.

To my colleagues at Drew University for ongoing support, and my beloved students, who change hearts and minds—including mine—with their artistry and bravery.

To Christopher Bakken and my Writing Workshops in Greece cohort: Ευχαριστώ.

Special shout-outs to artistic wizard Sunra Thompson and keen-eyed copyeditor Caitlin Van Dusen. Eleanor Taylor: thank you for the book-cover illustration of my dreams!

Mandy Medley: I appreciate you showing this book (and writer) so much love.

For reliable childcare that made productivity possible: the irreplaceable Nichol "Spicy" Mann and the Rosie/Malcolm Valdez Duo.

To my beloved Vs and first readers, Jane Rose Porter and Onnesha Roychoudhuri: we owe a lifetime debt to Nadine.

Shelly Oria, sister and sage: you have paved the way for me in countless ways, and תודה in every language will not suffice.

To my parents for nourishing and sustaining my dreams, and my other parents, Susan and Don, for their wide-open arms, and my siblings for decades of encouragement.

To anyone I may have missed and everyone who cheered me on: thank you.

To Jeremy, true partner and my favorite artist: this book is for you.

To Oliver Nathan and Leo Zachary: I love you more.

COURTNEY ZOFFNESS writes fiction and nonfiction. She won the Sunday Times Short Story Award, an Emerging Writer Fellowship from the Center for Fiction, the Susan Atefat Creative Nonfiction Prize from *Arts & Letters*, and artist residencies from MacDowell. Her work has appeared in the *Paris Review Daily*, the *Southern Review*, *Longreads*, and elsewhere, and her essays were listed as "Notable" in *Best American Essays* 2018 and 2019. She teaches at Drew University and lives with her family in Brooklyn, New York.